*The Experience
of Handicap*

The Experience of Handicap

David Thomas

Methuen

LONDON and NEW YORK

First published in 1982 by
Methuen & Co. Ltd
11 New Fetter Lane, London EC4P 4EE

Published in the USA by
Methuen & Co.
in association with Methuen, Inc.
733 Third Avenue, New York, NY 10017

© 1982 David Thomas

Photoset in Monophoto Apollo by
Servis Filmsetting Ltd, Manchester

Printed in Great Britain by
Richard Clay (The Chaucer Press) Ltd
Bungay, Suffolk

British Library Cataloguing in Publication Data
Thomas, David
    The experience of handicap.—(Education paperbacks)
    1. Handicapped
    I. Title
    362.4   HV1568

    ISBN 0-416-74710-8
    ISBN 0-416-74720-5 Pbk

Library of Congress Cataloging in Publication Data
Thomas, D. J. (David John), 1932–
    The experience of handicap.

    (Education paperbacks)
    Bibliography: p.
    Includes index.
    1. Handicapped   I. Title.
    HV1568.T48   362.4   81-22494
    ISBN 0-416-74710-8   AACR2
    ISBN 0-416-74720-5 (pbk)

Contents

Acknowledgements

I would like to offer my thanks to John Vaughan, Tutor-Librarian in the School of Education at the University of Liverpool, and all his colleagues for their skilled help, speedily and cheerfully given; to Andrew Craig of the British Epilepsy Association; to Pat Sumner and Chris Gerken for typing; to Margaret Hewitt and Chris Edgerton for openness and sharing; and to my family for their support and encouragement.

The author and publisher would like to thank the following for permission to reproduce copyright material: Jack Ashley and The Bodley Head for an extract from *Journey Into Silence*; G. Edwards and Granada Publishing Limited for an extract from *Keep in Touch*; A.M. Fox and Action Research for the Crippled Child for an extract from *They Get This Training But They Don't Really Know How You Feel*; Mrs Margaret Hewitt for an extract from *A Survey of the Experiences and Perceived Needs of Parents of Handicapped Children*; Miss Dorcas Munday for extracts from *Dorcas: Opportunity not Pity*; Edwin J. Thomas, the American Sociological Association and the *Journal of Health and Human Behavior* for extracts from *Problems of Disability from the Perspective of Role Theory*; M. Wallace and M. Robson and Times Books Limited for an extract from *On Giant's Shoulders*.

Introduction

In this book I have attempted to convey an impression of the experience of impairment, disability and handicap, and such an impression must be selective and hence partial. No single volume can do justice to the range of reactions, responses and events which might legitimately be included. In making a selection based on the accounts of people who have been or who are disabled, I have been influenced by a dislike of accounts which are blatantly sentimental or overtly propagandist , and attracted to those which in a sense demystify handicap. It is those people who show 'the disabled' as ordinary men and women facing up to extraordinary circumstances I find the most revealing. Professionals whose work brings them into contact with disabled people appear to have ambiguous attitudes to these personal histories; they are seen as 'unrepresentative', 'interesting' or 'unrealistic', either presenting a too gloomy or over-optimistic view, but seldom 'typical'. There is, of course, no typical or representative disabled person since the range and diversity of personalities, conditions and human and community resources imply greater rather than lesser heterogeneity. The accounts which I have read emphasize individuality rather than stereotypes. They speak of ordinary people discovering unknown qualities and reserves of personal strengths and depths of motivation and often surprising themselves. This is not a special quality of disabled people; to believe that would be to exchange one myth for another. It may be seen in all sorts of people in different circumstances when confronted with stress.

I have chosen to write through these personal and individual accounts, and this means that wider sociological perspectives have been somewhat neglected, but this is not to underestimate the view that disabled people have to contend with more than their physical status; they have to live with long developed structures in society which make their lives more difficult. People who are disabled, whatever the current rhetoric, do seem to suffer a measure of social ostracism, and are perceived to be on the 'abnormal' side of society; they are seen as 'the problem' and comparatively little attention is paid to the ways in which society prevents their access to a wide range of amenities, and limits opportunities which not only make social integration more problematic but prevent disabled people from showing their capacity to enrich our social fabric. Still too deeply embedded for comfort is the charitable, philanthropic, concessionary view, and rather low down on the value scale comes a notion like rights. Only when disabled people are active politically in the negoti- ation for their rightful place in society will their position improve.

Although written for teachers, social workers, care staff and others whose work brings them in touch with disabled people and their families, I hope that a wider readership will find in these accounts many points of contact. Though the primary emphasis is on the individual there is also a collective voice which expresses a shared humanity – this is the dynamic for future change.

Chapter 1 deals with various definitions and contrasts the factual and subjective sides of disability. Chapter 2 shows the important changes in attitudes that have taken place, while Chapter 3 illustrates the changes in 'identity' which can ac- company impairment. Chapter 4 discusses some of the features of interpersonal behaviour and Chapter 5 looks at the issue of care. Chapter 6 is the first of four on children and families, and deals with the birth of a handicapped child. Chapter 7 describes the relationship of parents with professional agencies, and Chapter 8 examines some of the minor and the more serious aspects of bringing up a handicapped child. Chapter 9 looks at the world of the handicapped child. Finally Chapter 10 suggests that our society manufactures handicap and discusses how we might change this.

1
Impairment, disability and handicap

Disablement has many facets: medical, economic, legal and bureaucratic. It has a psychological face (the impact of disability upon the individual person); a socio-psychological side (the valence of disability in social behaviour) and the sociological dimension (role, status, normative framework, and sub-cultural features). Each facet contributes to the total image of disability. We have a convenient visual shorthand for the image of disability – the logo of the pin-figure in a wheelchair which appears on car stickers, access and facilities signs. The diversity and range of people represented by this logo have been simplified into a unitary visual concept. In the accounts given by disabled people we may rediscover the human being so abstracted.

Whatever the logo may imply, the most significant feature of disablement is its diversity. Not only do we have differences of causation, type of impairment, severity and prognosis, the condition spans the entire age-range and is no respecter of race, sex or social class; there are also important differences between acquired and life-long disabilities. Equally varied are the responses to disability which produce not a unitary but a variegated picture. Within the world of disabilities we can find contradictory images of success and failure, optimism and pessimism, tragedy and humour, 'matter of fact' reactions and pathological responses, acceptance and stigma, recognition of individual differences and stereotyping, superb support services and inadequate ones, sensible and silly legislation, community support and social isolation, resignation and rebellion, successful careers and appalling job prospects, deeply satisfying personal relationships and loneliness, acceptance and rejection.

As varied as the individual disabled person's condition and reaction are public responses, from 'they're just like everyone else', imaginative concern, mawkish sentimentality, indifference, rejection and hostility.

In addition to the variety of individual differences in the population of disabled people the social and psychological environment is constantly changing. One aspect of change is that which has occurred in the history of provision services, benefits and legal rights. Blaxter (1976), reviewing these changes, noted two trends in the evolution of affirmative legislation and social policy, which are not always in harmony – humanitarian and economic factors. The earliest provisions arose out of charitable activities on behalf of the 'innocently' disabled and those with visible impairments. The blind, the deaf, and the orthopaedically handicapped child were among the first to be singled out. Later this aid was extended to the war-disabled and the industrially-disabled, and in turn was widened to include the chronically ill. She describes this process as a progressive 'loosening and widening' of the definition of disability. With the widening definition and the availability of more and more services to more and more categories of disability, the economic cost of such services became (and is) a constant factor in policy-making. The growth of a comprehensive welfare service could not have taken place without producing awkward questions of definition for doctors as well as bureaucrats, a conflict of 'unavoidable incompatibilities between medical definition systems, which ideally are individual, qualified and provisional and administrative categories which are necessarily rigid, dichotomous and designed for large groups of people' (Blaxter, 1976: 10).

Disability is not only a matter of medical and administrative definition, it is a personal one of how each person with an impairment defines him- or herself. Both official and subjective definitions (and the social and personal consequences of such definitions) may place an individual in a position where taken-for-granted identities are subject to transformation. Berger and Luckmann's (1971) view of marginality introduces the idea that a person whose normality of social identity is fragile and negotiable may occupy a position which is uncertain, ambiguous and not fully institutionalized, being at a distance from what most people would regard as society's core institutions and values. To some extent this is the position of disabled people, for though they are not separate from society they appear to occupy a marginal position, uneasily situated between a rigid dichotomous social classification and undifferentiated 'normality'.

Just as there are many facets of disability there is also no single vantage point. The nature and meaning of disability change with perceptions from the public view, the professional view and the insiders' view — that provided by disabled people themselves. There is one view of disability to which we are all exposed, irrespective of our personal contact with disabled people: that is the impression or image used by fund raisers. Charitable appeals unequivocally state that people with x, y or z handicap have needs which are beyond those provided for by the State. Such appeals imply that the recipients of charity are worthy of the act. Those charged with fund-raising produce a specialized image of disability nicely calculated to evoke an impression of dependency, need and worth. The blind judo expert, packaged as 'He's good, he's blind, he's trained', manages to combine moral worth, compassion and value for money in one slogan. But we can ask if the image used by the fund-raiser is a true image of the particular handicap. The visually handicapped old lady shuffling around a geriatric ward may be as valid if less appealing an image. The use of personable paraplegic or appealing (sic) mentally handicapped toddlers may be images at variance with the modal characteristics of the groups they purport to represent. The high incidence of handicaps among the middle aged and elderly may be obscured from public appreciation; isolated examples of disabled people running a complex business using the wizardry of the microchip may present a discrepant view of the job prospects for the majority of disabled people. Equally misleading in their own way are the heroic examples such as Ann Sullivan and Helen Keller where the outstanding achievements of an individual have become more than just a shining example and have become a placebo, for if such achievements are possible for some, then all that can be holding back other equally handicapped people is lack of ability or insufficient motivation! The view you have depends on where you stand.

So far we have used the terms impairment, disability and handicap. These are sometimes used interchangeably and now require to be defined.

Definitions

Among the terms most frequently used by professionals are impairment, disability and handicap and although there are differences of opinions over definition and usage, there is a measure of consensus over the need to divide or categorize the disabled population as an aid to inter-disciplinary communication.

Impairment

Impairment has been defined as an 'anatomical, pathological or psychological disorder' which is defined and described symptomatically or diagnostically (Garrad, 1974: 142). Impairments may affect locomotion, motor activities, sensory systems, and be medically based or of psychological origin. A more concise definition is 'any loss of psychological, physiological or anatomical structure or function' (Bury, 1979: 36). Impairments may be permanent or temporary, be present from birth or acquired adventitiously. It is appropriate to regard the term impairment as a neutral or objective description of the site, nature and severity of loss of functional capacity. An example of this would be the graph produced as the result of audiometric testing in which hearing loss and residual capacity for sound detection are objectively expressed.

Disability

Disability refers to the impact of impairment upon the performance of activities commonly accepted as the basic elements of everyday living – walking, negotiating stairs, getting in and out of bed, dressing, feeding, using the lavatory, bathing, holding down a job or just being able to carry on a conversation. Disability can be used when an impairment, objectively defined, constitutes a hindrance to mobility, domestic routines, or occupational and communication skills.

Handicap

Handicap is a term which has come to represent the more profound effects of impairments and disabilities which implicate the whole person and not just selective incapacities. Handicap in children has been seen as an impairment or a disability which 'for a substantial period or permanently, retards, disturbs or otherwise adversely affects normal growth, development and adjustment to life' (*Court Report*, 1976: 219) and in adults 'constitutes a disadvantage for a given individual in that it limits or prevents the fulfilment of a role that is normal (depending on age, sex and social and cultural factors) for that individual' (Bury, 1979: 36). Handicap is therefore an evaluatory concept in which the interaction of impairment and disability with an individual's psychological make-up, the resources available, and social attitudes affects adversely the performance of ordinary roles. Handicap is a value-judgement applied by others to an impaired-disabled person on the basis of failure to perform customary social roles; and of course, this value-judgement the impaired-disabled person may apply to him- or herself, or vigorously reject. To move from impairment to handicap is to cover the distance from symptoms to social role. It is also to move from objectivity to subjectivity.

Figure 1   Three basic terms

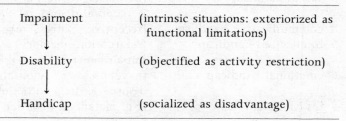

Impairment	(intrinsic situations: exteriorized as functional limitations)
Disability	(objectified as activity restriction)
Handicap	(socialized as disadvantage)

Source: Bury, 1979: 37.

The presence of impairment does not necessarily imply disability and neither does disability imply handicap. On the other hand it is possible for impairment to lead to disablement or handicap, for two people with broadly similar functional limitations may face objectively similar activity restrictions, but one may retain his conventional social roles (albeit somewhat modified) while the other, with different resources (personal or community), may cast himself or be cast as a handicapped person. 'Some people in wheelchairs succeed in working and maintaining a high level of independence whilst others require a high degree of nursing care. Disability is therefore to some extent self-defined' (Lees and Shaw, 1974: 5), as it is with handicap.

Whilst professionals may agree on the value of a precise vocabulary, the niceties of the distinctions have probably not permeated far beyond the professional pale. It is interesting to note that these terms may carry different connotations among those with impairments. For example, the competitor at a sports meeting for disabled people rejected the term disabled and said 'I may be handicapped but disabled – never!' These terms carry not only precise clinical meanings but have a strong affective element.

A widely used system of classifying disabilities was drawn up by Dr Agerholm in 1973. Designed to improve the quality of statistical information collected by the Department of Employment, it became part of the case made to drop the practice of recording statistics using the clinical cause of the impairment. The main divisions of the classifying system were

1	locomotion handicap	(mobility, posture, manipulation)
2	visceral handicap	(ingestion, excretion)
3	visual handicap	(loss of sight, partial loss, perceptual disorders)
4	communicative handicap	(receptive, expressive)
5	intellectual handicap	(retardation, memory impairment)
6	emotional handicap	(psychoses, behavioural disorders, drug addiction)
7	invisible handicap	(e.g. metabolic disorder, epilepsy, etc.)
8	visible handicap	(e.g. skin disorders, scar)

Numbers

Data which have been collected using clinical causation of impairments–disability not only include the frequency of occurrence of conditions, but also the range of severity of impairments associated with that condition. (Harris (1971) used a 1–8 scale for severity of handicap (1–3: very severe, 4–6: severe to appreciable, 7–8: minimal or no handicap).)

Harris used the following broad categories of clinical conditions: infective and parasitic diseases, neoplasms, allergies, nutritional diseases, diseases of the blood, mental, neurotic and personality disorders, diseases of the central nervous system (polio, cerebral haemorrhage, strokes, multiple sclerosis, Parkinson's disease, cerebral palsy, head injuries, etc.), diseases of the circulatory system, respiratory system, digestive system, genito-urinary system, sense organs (excluding blindness), skin and cellular tissue, diseases of bones and conditions which affect mobility, congenital malformations, injuries, senility, amputations and blindness.

The conditions included in Harris's survey all show a range of severity. Among those conditions with high percentages in the 1–3 category (very severe) we find cerebral haemorrhage and strokes, multiple sclerosis, Parkinson's disease, cerebral palsy and senility. To illustrate the range of severity we can take a few examples.

Table 1 Severity of handicaps (percentages)

	1–3	4	5	6	7	8
Cerebral palsy	15·9	3·2	4·8	20·6	22·2	33·3
Sense organs	0·9	1·5	5·0	18·0	17·3	57·3
Blindness	5·4	3·2	6·4	11·5	18·9	54·7

Source: Harris, 1971: 230.

Combining categories 1–6 (very severe–appreciable) we find that 44·5 per cent of people with cerebral palsy are affected to an appreciable or greater degree by this condition, while those with affected sense organs or blindness are affected to a similar degree at 25·4 and 26·5 per cent levels.

Harris also has information on the age distribution of severity of handicaps. In the 16–29 age group in the 1–3 category, there were an estimated 5000 people, rising to 12,000 in the 30–49 age group, 26,000 in the 50–64 group, 35,000 in the 65–74 age group and 80,000 in the 75 and over age group; whilst in the 4–5 category the estimate was 4000, 30,000, 94,000, 102,000 and 125,000. This illustrates that the propagandist image of disability centred on children and young people is contradicted by the actual age distribution of disability. The age spread and the variety of conditions and the range of severity of handicaps should serve as a reminder that in using words such as *disabled people*, there is a danger of thinking of them as a collectivity.

> The most important aspect of definition, however, for all who deal in schemes of social aid which aim to assist people with handicaps either in cash or in kind, is that 'the handicapped' make up a group which is not in the least homogeneous. People with handicaps, so often discussed as an entity, are in many ways *less* alike than are able-bodied people. There is little in common between the special needs of a wheelchair-bound but articulate person who is able to work and some one mentally handicapped from birth and hence unable to fight his own battles or provide and administer his own finance, or between the armless teenager, part of whose problem is to fend off excessive 'sympathy', and the middle-aged woman with emphysema or epilepsy who meets with hostility or lack of understanding because she has no *visible* handicap. The problems of a blind person are different from those of the many for whom blindness is part of a complex of sensory handicaps that have come with age, and the problems of the deaf, the agoraphobic and those of exceptionally small stature are each different again. (Simkins and Tickner, 1978: 16)

However, there is a sense in which a measure of homogeneity may be imputed to the handicapped in Britain. That homogeneity may be described as 'disadvantage'. The extent of this disadvantage can be expressed in the following way: about 25 per cent of the disabled population *surrender a major proportion of their personal independence* (unable to dress or have a bath unaided); and about 13 per cent are *chair, bed or house bound*; approximately 24 per cent are forced into *premature retirement*; while 21 per cent face a *loss of social integration* through living alone. As for the *economic consequences* of disability, the median weekly income of disabled people is thought to be about half that of the general population, and one source claims that between 0·8 and 0·9 million of the 1·2 million disabled people in Britain are living in poverty or on the margins of poverty. Among the other disadvantages faced by disabled people we may list housing, transportation, access to public buildings, career opportunities, recreational facilities, as well as perhaps more intractable issues relating to attitudes. Many of these issues will be discussed in a later chapter.

The concept of disadvantage allows us to appreciate that disability should be perceived as a relationship. That impairments can lead to disabilities and handicaps is in part a function of a society which is organized and structured for and on behalf of the dominant able-bodied. Disability is not the 'attribute of an individual but the outcome of an oppressive relationship between people with physical impairments and the rest of society' (Finkelstein, 1980: 47). Definitions of impairment, disability and handicap are inadequate if they present these conditions as residing in the person alone. The meaning of these terms becomes more comprehensive and complex when they are perceived as a relationship between individuals and groups and society as a whole. Impairment can be seen as personal misfortune but disability and handicap are, from this viewpoint, secondary and tertiary over-lays – the product of the values, attitudes and behaviours of the dominant segment of society which tends to exclude impaired people from the mainstream of life. To cite the disadvantages experienced by many disabled people, their dependency upon others or upon technology is not to suggest that these make them unique. There are many other sections of society who are disadvanaged and dependent, and indeed only a moment's reflection will show that interdependency is axiomatic for most of us. What is needed, as Finkelstein suggests, is a perspective which does not constantly evaluate the disabled person's differential from the able-bodied functioning, but as norm-free independent people who can challenge the 'material and social environment's capacity to satisfy their needs' (Finkelstein, 1980: 38). This would mean shifting questions like 'What is it about disabled people that prevents them from working?' to 'How do our transport system, building access, education, training, factory machinery prevent impaired people from working?' Clearly such a perspective represents a radical shift with the potential for re-examining the nature of impairment.

Social group or social category

So far we have noted some of the broad features of the *objective context* of disability – the hard data on incidence, age distribution of handicap and the economic facts surrounding disability. Co-existing with this objective context is a *subjective context* and this refers to the personal experiences of disabled people, their attitudes, the attitudes they experience and the meaning that lay and professional people attach to concepts of handicap. As the Simkins and Tickner (above) quotation shows, the population of handicapped people is composed of individuals with very different needs, problems and resources. Is it at all possible then to conceive 'the handicapped' or 'the disabled' as some kind of distinctive entity? Or to express it another way, are disabled people members of a social category or of a social group?

One way of considering any complex society like our own is to see it as a mosaic of social groups – ethnic, occupational, religious, political. And can we add 'the disabled' as one such group? It is a commonplace of the literature on the handicapped to liken those so labelled to ethnic minority groups having a low or devalued status, subject to discrimination and being denied opportunities customarily available to members of the majority group. Accord-ing to Tajfel (1978) a central factor in minority-group membership is a common element of 'awareness'; of knowing that one does *belong* to the group and sharing with other group members a collective awareness of the stereotypes held about group mem-bers. Group members are sensitized to the socially relevant characteristics which separate them from the majority and which bind them together.

Tajfel makes clear that conditions like stammering, red hair or obesity are examples of individual differences which do not result in group 'awareness'.

> These characteristics, although shared by a large number of people, retain their *individual* significance in a person's life. It would be difficult to think of 'group' social consequences following upon obesity, lefthandedness or stammering. Ob-viously, any of these individual features can acquire enormous importance in a person's life; and just as obviously, they may create for such people a number of social handicaps. (Tajfel, 1978: 5)

To simplify social life we use a variety of social categories (putting people into classes, groups, types and kinds) and from these categories we draw inferences about people even when we know little about them except their categorical characteristics. Such inferences are used to explain people's behaviour, to make predictions about behaviour, and to reinforce our perceptions of our place in the general social order. For Tajfel the differences between an individual attribute and a group characteristic is that in the former the individual attribute is not used as a basis for making further social inferences where as in the latter it is.

> 'Fatness' or 'stammering' or 'small stature' are not used as criteria in a social typology. Socially relevant characteristics of other people who share the same attribute are randomly related to that attribute; in other words, they have very limited implications for the social attributes of others who share the same characteristics. (ibid.: 5)

Those with common characteristics may share, as individuals, a common stereotype even if they do not present themselves as members of a group, as in popular views about fat people. Clearly there is a difference between physical disability and ethnic minority membership and an individual disabled person may not regard him- or herself as a member of a group, although they may evoke stereotypic responses in others. But the current picture is not as clear cut as the distinction between social category and social group may suggest, for in recent years we have seen something like the emergence of group feeling, solidarity and awareness among people who are disabled which have many of the features of a social group. The administration of special services for disabled people, specific ministerial responsibility, legislation, directional and access signs, the Olympic Games for disabled people and their own International Year and various pressure groups, all point to the growth of something like collective awareness. Some sections of the disabled population have gone further down this particular road than others, as for example the National Union of the Deaf which has advocated far-reaching reforms in the teaching of deaf children and which has a real sense of sub-cultural identity (NUD, 1978). Similarly the growth of group feelings among disabled people was illustrated by public meetings held to encourage central government action for the reduction of handicaps through improved pre- and post-natal services; at these meetings significant numbers of disabled people participated. Such political activity is of a different order from social gatherings of people with similar disabilities – once described by the NUD as 'banding together in hostility against the hearing world'. It is the beginning of a group identity, as yet perhaps not particularly potent but becoming so and from which will emerge a self-generated vision of change and development.

To deviate from the norm

If we regard people who are disabled as belonging to a social category, then how is membership of that category determined? There appears to be a number of ways in which people can be seen as atypical, exceptional or unusual. In psychology, measures of intelligence applied to a representative sample of the population produce a frequency curve along which individuals can be allocated such descriptions as 'within the average range', 'exceptionally intelligent' or 'sub-normal intelligence'. Equally in the physical domain, measurement can lead to descriptions such as 'above average height' or 'overweight'. These statistical devices have their uses, not only in providing clothing and shoe manufacturers with useful information about which sizes are going to reach the widest market, but in medicine, insurance and many branches of ergonomics.

There is another sense in which departure from the norm is perceived in the everyday world. It is as though we carry about with us our own in-built set of tables and curves which enable us to detect and catalogue significant (to us) inter-individual differences, such as tall-short, fat-thin, beautiful-ugly, black-white, and physically normal-physically different.

This perceptual awareness may have its roots in some ancestral memory when it was vitally important to distinguish others from our own kind – a sort of visual Shibboleth. Some have suggested the alertness to visual deformity is of genetic origin – a Darwinian sorting process for selecting fit from unfit mates but these ideas are no more than vague speculations. Whatever the underlying mechanism, social training makes sure that each generation acquires the ground rules for perceptions of significant differences. The social importance of extreme variations in appearance and physique is shown by the positive and negative values which are attached to such departures from the norm and these values are acquired through an unconscious learning process. It is this process which enables us to define others as exceptional, atypical or non-normal: it also provides us with a definition of what it is to be normal.

This sorting process may carry only minor social or personal penalties for the individual, but it can imply severe censure. What seems to happen is that the visible signs of distinctiveness are used to imply additional qualities and characteristics which in turn are used as the basis for interactional, emotional and evaluative responses. One of the best examples of how stock expectations can be generated on the basis of physical stigmata is mongolism or Down's Syndrome. There is a measure of agreement between professionals and lay people about the personality of the child with Down's Syndrome — affable, mischievous, docile, affectionate, pleasing, but also stubborn and self-willed. For Langdon Down in the nineteenth century, these traits were the residue of the behaviour of man's remote ancestors. In spite of studies which have shown something of the variety of personality in this syndrome, the conviction of a common basis of behaviour survives.

There is a compelling impression of characteristic developmental stages for personality in this syndrome. In caricature, the placid, sensorially insufficient infant becomes an emotionally intact and outgoing child who turns subsequently into a sullen adolescent and finally faces premature ageing and marked behavioural deterioration in early adulthood. *But not always and may be not even in the majority of cases.* (my italics) (Gibson, 1978: 148)

Gibson even suggests that the existence of stereotypic views may have actually encouraged the evolution of 'traits' which are regarded as 'characteristic' of the syndrome by a kind of self-fulfilling prophecy: the stereotype has become authentic. Similar perceptions may be at work in the case of other disabilities. Blindness and deafness seem to evoke specific (though very different) responses (Lukoff, 1972).

Obviously variations in appearance, physique and functional effectiveness have their positive and negative sides; the person with a beautiful face, the athlete or dancer is admired, while facial disfigurement, obesity and physical handicaps evoke opposite emotions. The tracing of the development of these value-beliefs is not our concern for the moment, except to note the strength of these negative values, which may be illustrated by the case of a man who posed as a disabled person and gained some distinction as a performer in sports for paraplegics – a rare and curious example of someone wishing to cross over the normal-disabled divide. How do we regard his action? What satisfaction can be obtained by competing with disabled people? We find his behaviour a puzzle.

What is the function of this sensitivity to the appearance of others, this capacity to distinguish 'normal' from 'handicap'? We know that in the world of the young child differences in appearances, behaviour and intelligence are of great significance. The Opies, in their *Lore and Language of School Children*, record the schoolchildren's taunts at the fat child – 'rubber-guts, slob, slug, ten-ton', and for girls 'Tubelina'; while 'skinnies' get similar treatment, 'Bony marony, broomstick, needle legs' and 'fat as a matchstick with the wood shaved off'. Those below average height are 'squirts, ankle biters, half-pints or Goliaths'; red-haired children are greeted with 'ginger conk, ginger nuts, red-head and rusty', while those with freckles or glasses have their special terms. If you're too bright you're a 'clever dick', not bright enough and you are 'bats, crackers, daffy or dippy'.

A similar process is carried on in adulthood. Although the vocabulary of distinctiveness becomes more subtle, its essential function is to provide an affirmation of normality by marking out what is not. It is as though we acquire a drive to reassure ourselves of our rightful place among the unstigmatized. Our culture teaches us what are the signs and symbols of what is normal and that awareness is built-in. Although we would perhaps be hard put to define the parameters of this process there are obvious 'signs' such as gender, race and social class. While such reactions are most obviously seen in respect of visible handicaps, they extend to those handicaps which are not immediately apparent and perceptual awareness influences behaviour, which in turn affects perceptual awareness.

Handicapped identity

To be perceived as a handicapped person is to experience a

distinct social status. These perceptions and the values associated with them give meaning to being handicapped, and such meaning appears to involve feelings and styles of behaviour which provide the handicapped person with clues to his social and personal worth. Attitudes evoked by handicaps may be seen in everyday interactions as well as in structural features, such as legislation, provision and services, and these attitudes appear to vary between handicaps. While attitudes to disability are undergoing change, such changes may be little more than a modification of surface features without fundamental alteration and the attitudes experienced by disabled people offer useful guidelines to one important set of dominant value-systems in our society: power, prestige, influence and attractiveness.

If we regard the handicapped identity as one confirmed upon a person by reason of his or her physical/functional difference (an identity which may or may not be accepted by the individual concerned), an important part of that identity is conveyed by signs of ambiguity and unease. The disabled person represents some kind of challenge to taken-for-granted assumptions about what it means to be human. The disabled person is seen as a 'problem' at the level of everyday intercourse and makes for uncertainty about moral worth as judged by the criteria that provide certainty about position, prestige and power. Is an imbecile child of greater value to society than a well-trained sheepdog? What is the point of keeping a road accident victim on a life-support system for years on end? What is the value of providing for the care of a paralyzed person who will always require care and attention simply to stay alive in the technical sense? Why should we go to the expense of adapting our local library so that one or two people in wheelchairs can have access? Surely it is better to kill (sorry, allow to die) infants with congenital malformations since we can predict that the 'quality of life' for such children will be impoverished?

These difficult questions are just some of the problematic issues these disabilities evoke. Similar ambiguities arise in the area of the interpretation of the behaviour of disabled people. For example, we read an account of a woman paralyzed as the result of a road accident: she gets married, brings up three children, runs a home, qualifies as an architect, manages a successful practice and finds time to act as a spokesperson for others similarly handicapped.

How do we respond to this story? With admiration certainly, but then if this picture of her life is *so* positive has she left something out? Do we not almost expect that there would be some bitterness, some sense of the tragedy of her situation? We read her story again and this time it becomes possible to perceive that this is not an autobiography but propaganda; for such energy, achievement and happiness could not be natural. Here psychology comes to our rescue for such a powerful drive *must* be a form of over-compensation. Other explanations evoke an even more dangerous concept: that of the exceptional person with exceptional gifts – a variant on the theme that each handicap brings 'compensating' advantages. One further response to her story could come from the hardened professional with his 'very interesting, but highly untypical; you should see the ones on my caseload – they *are* handicapped'.

However the person's behaviour and motives are explained, they will be explained *through* the handicap in an inevitable causal chain: success will be because of the handicap and so will failure. This causal chain is now almost axiomatic among lay and professionals alike. The handicapped identity is seen as the central organizing factor around which explanations of the person are constructed, a construction prejudicial to people so perceived and which neglects the weight to be given to the relationship between the person and society.

If this is the case, the disabled are particularly *vulnerable* since all their behaviours, attitudes and feelings are interpreted within a special frame of reference. They are likely to be described and evaluated by different standards, criteria and rules of evidence from those which apply in normal social behaviour. This vulnerability extends beyond the disabled person to those in close and regular contact with him or her. Parents of handicapped children are liable to have their actions interpreted through their child's disability. A newspaper article gave the story of a family who were carrying out an intensive programme of patterning (putting the child through a complex series of movements) with their brain-damaged child and this programme involved a number of friends and relatives who worked with the child eight hours a day for seven days a week. Letters in the same newspaper a week later carried contrasting views: either splendid devotion and commitment, or massive guilt-wracked over-compensation.

These differing sets of attitudes are typical of the variations in viewpoints to which disabled people are subjected and which leave them vulnerable to a range of attitudes which cannot be readily predicted.

From the other side

At the beginning of this chapter it was suggested that images of disability are formed from many sources – the media, personal and professional contacts. The health, care and welfare of handicapped people have resulted in a proliferation of professional specialists (as well as a considerable number of concerned volunteers) and each professional group has its area of expertise and territory, such as speech therapy, occupational therapy, mobility training, social work, rehabilitation, medicine and teaching. One of the effects of professional compartmentalization is to make handicaps a *professional problem* which can only be fully understood by those who have been trained in a certain way.

Each professional group – doctors, health visitors, etc. – has its own value-system, technical language and techniques, and within each defined territory there is a built-in tendency to reify its activities and to enlarge its mysteries, making the business of dealing with the handicapped a highly differentiated and specialized service. Since professionals are most interested in communicating with other professionals, we see the growth of shared values and attitudes within a professional group which has the effect of creating an image of work demanding special skills (which indeed may be so), but in the welter of inter-professional communication the view from the other side is not always highly regarded.

The views of people who have been through the professional process are sometimes treated as useful, supplementary anecdotal material or rejected as being too subjective and personalized, lacking research rigour or simply dismissed as the outpouring of an atypical or highly disaffected individual. In seeking to present some examples of views from the other side, I have tried to maintain a balance of opinion showing both the positive and negative sides of the experience of disabled people. What I hope these excerpts show is that behind the jargon of the professional there are ordinary men and women whose lives and experiences are open to us without the intrusive veil of professional interpretation, and we do not require the recondite vocabulary of specialists to share in those experiences. This is to argue for the de-mystification of handicap; to opt for a view of handicapped people as highly varied and uniquely individual rather than as category exemplars of the heroic or the pathetic. Of course such a view exacts a penalty. If our perceptions are to be grounded in reality the non-handicapped will have to give up illusions, and the handicapped will have to give up their status as a protected species: not the abandonment of affirmative policies, care or concern, but a willingness to see those with disabilities as citizens with natural rights, entitled to have their physical and social world modified to meet their needs and an interpersonal environment that stops regarding them as exceptional.

Summary

Impairment, disability and handicap are complex personal and social states which contain many contradictions. These states are not static since changes occur within the life-style of the person, while attitudes to impaired and disabled people are also in the process of change. Since the beginning of a social welfare policy towards disabled people there has been a progressive widening and loosening of definitions of these conditions. The importance of definitions has become greater as access to significant services depends upon such definitions. Public images of the disabled population are created by various sources – the media, fund-raisers and by disabled people themselves – and there may be discrepant messages between the public image of disability and those employed by the image-makers. Impairment, disability and handicap used to be seen as terms representing a continuum from objective descriptions of functional limitations to social disadvantage. The varied and individual nature of this population was emphasized although their collective disadvantage was stressed through the repressive nature of the relationship between the disabled and the rest of society. One of the paradoxes of the disabled population is that in order to achieve their rights, to obtain their independence and to achieve social integration, it is necessary for them to assert a collective power and influence.

2
Attitudes

An attitude is an acquired orientation towards or away from some object, person, group, event or idea. It is a disposition more enduring than mood yet capable under certain circumstances of being modified or even reversed. Attitudes seem to have certain features, such as a cognitive component (how a person explains, justifies or rationalizes his views), a behavioural component (how a person behaves when confronted by the object, event or person which evokes a particular attitude) and an affective component which is the emotions aroused by the object, person or event associated with an attitude. Attitudes may be acquired through conscious socialization or unconsciously as in some forms of extreme racial prejudice where the individual experiences un-acknowledged feelings of personal inadequacy which are dis-placed on to members of a social group over whom he may enjoy illusory but satisfying feelings of superiority. Some attitudes are shaped by membership of powerful social groups where member-ship is conditional upon accepting group values; others may be acquired through a single dramatic or traumatic experience. Attitudes can also be acquired via a non-conscious absorption of ideas which are, as it were, 'in the air', not formally taught but caught, as for example the way in which the women's movement has alerted us to the extent to which masculine values pervade our language and thinking.

Attitudes and handicap

It is not possible to be precise about the origins of attitudes to handicapped people. Among the suggestions that have been made is that primitive man lived in an environment that placed a premium on survival skills and had no margin for the support of the weak and the helpless. With the growth of settled com-

21

munities producing an economic surplus the possibilities for the incapacitated to be supported and to make a modest contribution to social life became feasible. If survival became possible, acceptance was more problematic and we had to wait until the time of Galen, Hippocrates and Aristotle for the first attempts to understand disability without invocation of sinister and demoniacal explanations. Aristotle saw the problem of deaf people as exclusion from the central process in learning – human speech; while Hippocrates and Galen interpreted epilepsy as a disturbance of the normal process of the mind. To this strand of scientific interest we must add the later charitable view of the Christian faith with its belief in the value of kindness and good works which must have alleviated the condition of the blind and halt, if it did nothing for their social status. According to Bowe (1978) the spirit of naturalistic inquiry begun in Greece was delayed a thousand years, and in medieval Europe supernatural explanations of disability abounded. Disability was a source of fear and ridicule, persecution and mockery. Haffter (1968) points out that in the middle ages there was a pervasive belief that deformed infants were 'changelings' substituted for the 'real' child by envious creatures, and since the changeling was not a human child, barbarous practices were legitimized in attempts to affect a recovery of the real child. At the time of Martin Luther the birth of a handicapped child was accepted as proof that the parents were involved in witchcraft, impious practices, or simply had wicked thoughts and in the *Malleus Maleficarum* of 1487 deformed children were regarded as the fruit of sexual intercourse between a woman and the devil. In the notes of guidance on questions to be asked during the examination of witches, one was on whether she had given birth to a changeling.

The transformation of the idea of the changeling within the framework of Christian demonology showed a shift from projection to the relatively harmless or even benevolent 'good people' to the unequivocally wicked devil. He was the instrument of a vengeful God. The blame for what happened was internalized: diabolism, superstition and unbelief were at first generally regarded as sins of the parents which were punished by the child being stolen and another put in its place. Finally the fault was seen with even greater clarity to be a sin in thought against the child: if before or after its birth the parents cursed the child and wished the devil would take it, then the devil would do precisely that. The deformed or otherwise abnormal child now became a cause of great fear and pangs of conscience: 'have we offended against God?' It also became a shameful stigma in the eyes of society and a reason for isolation, ostracism and even persecution. (Haffter, 1968: 60–1)

These beliefs survived into the nineteenth century, and it may be suggested that even today remnants of these attitudes survive in a muted form.

In Tudor and Stuart England popular attitudes can be revealed, as they have been by Keith Thomas, through an examination of joke books of the period. While such books contain many stock characters which we can readily appreciate – foreigners, cuckolds, academics, scolding wives, the clergy, lawyers and so on – there were also a great many about physical deformity:

every disability, from idiocy to insanity to diabetes and bad breath, was a welcome source of amusement. 'We jest at a man's body that is not well proportioned,' said Thomas Wilson . . . 'and laugh at his countenance if . . . it be not comely by nature.' A typical Elizabethan joke book contains 'merry jests of fools', and 'merry jests of blind folk', while some of the trickster's pranks are brutal in the extreme. Such humour reflected the actual practice of a world where most professions were closed to the physically deformed, where visits to Bedlam were a standard form of entertainment and where idiots were maintained in noble households for amusement's sake. . . . At the lower social level we recall John Bunyan's account of the ale-house keeper who kept his poor idiot son, Edward, to entertain his guests 'by his foolish words and gestures'. (Thomas, 1977: 80–1)

But it was not only at the level of everyday life that deformity was an occasion for ridicule; it was also a fit subject for speculation by the best stocked mind of the age. 'Deformed persons, and eunuchs, and old men and bastards are envious. For he that cannot possibly mend his own case will do what he can to impair another', wrote Bacon in his *Essay on Envy*, but added, 'except that the defect light upon a very brave or heroic nature that thinketh to make his natural wants part of his honour.' Bacon shared a common view of his time 'For the natural lineaments of the body show the general inclination and disposition of the mind', an idea given dramatic form in Shakespeare's *Richard III* and his *Julius Caesar*.

Not all disabilities were seen as objectionable for while Pope's kyphosis could be described as

> Megre and worn and steeple crown'd,
> His visage long and shoulders round,
> His crippled corpse two spindle pegs
> Support, instead of human legs.

Milton's blindness seems to have conferred upon him, according to his contemporaries, some additional qualities of perception and wisdom.

From the rough and ready attitudes of Tudor and Stuart times to our present gentler manners is a remarkable social transformation. Keith Thomas notes that by the

> end of the seventeenth century, the doctrine that human weakness was no subject for laughter had taken hold of much of middle-class opinion: and it helped to produce the sentimental and humanitarian movement of the eighteenth century. The practice of keeping idiots declined sharply in the late Stuart age, out of the growing conviction . . . 'that it was unnatural to laugh at the natural' . . . But among the common people these new attitudes were slower to take root. . . . As for the softening of laughter, the discontinuance of the household fool and the banning of jokes about madness or physical deformity, we approach an area which has not lost its sensitivity. For there are some matters which even *we* regard as privileged from jest. (ibid.: 81)

As an example of someone at the turning point of this new sensitivity we can take the story of William Hay.

William Hay

William Hay was born in 1695 and in every respect bar one he might stand as a portrait of a typical gentleman of his time. He was a country squire, a justice of the peace, and a member of

Parliament. He was a cultivated and well-travelled man sharing the cultural, social and intellectual inclinations of his class. He led a quiet, useful existence in comfortable circumstances, with just enough eminence to make a minor entry in the *National Dictionary of Biography*. What makes Hay of interest to us is the essay he wrote in the year before his death in 1755, *Deformity*. This was a subject he could write on with some authority for he describes himself thus:

> If any reader imagines that a Print of me in the Frontispiece of this Work would give him a clearer idea of the subject, I have no objection; providing he will be at the Expense of ingraving. But for want of it, let him know; that I am scarce five feet high: that my back was bent in my Mother's womb.

In this essay he describes his childhood, his experiences in polite and not so polite society, and offers many philosophical speculations about deformity. He points out that to be deformed is to be singular.

> Bodily deformity is so rare: and therefore a Person so distinguished must naturally think, that he has had ill-luck in a Lottery, where there are about a Thousand prizes to one Blank. Among 558 Gentlemen in the Houses of Commons I am the only one that is so.

His aim in writing the essay was to range over the many questions that deformity raised, and to discuss in a philosophic vein the issues which would be of value to others 'oddly distinguished' and entertaining to the rest. He tried, so he said, to anatomize himself by offering on display his mental and physical imperfection and by elegant prose to produce a 'finished piece to atone for an ill-turned Person'. He acknowledged his good fortune at being born in an age which did not practise infanticide on deformed children and recalls with affection the care of his parents. These early years were difficult and left their mark, for though attempts were made to correct the curvature of his spine ('out of Tenderness tried every Art to correct the Errors of Nature') they were unsuccessful. He mildly chastizes his parents for the way they brought him up for they

> taught me to be ashamed of my Person, instead of arming me with true Fortitude to despise and Ridicule or Contempt of it.

> This caused me much uneasiness in my younger Days and it required many Years to conquer this Weakness: Of which I hope now there are but little Remains left.

He seems to have been convinced that his experiences as a child left a durable impression making him bashful, uneasy and unsure of himself. He notes that he was extremely sensitive about his personal appearance (but concludes so also were most men and women) and repeatedly acknowledges his gratitude in being born into that segment of society, 'the better part of Mankind', where politeness and good manners prevented any gentleman worthy of the name from commenting on his appearance.

This did not inhibit close friends from teasing him – a mark of kindness, affection and comradeship.

> I should be unfit to sit at Table with him should I resent his congratulations on my emerging from an Eclipse of a Sirloin of Roast Beef, or a Bowl of Punch, that stood between us.

The general high standard of manners and the gentle teasing of close friends were in marked contrast to the behaviour of the lower orders where 'Insolence grows in proportion as the man sinks in condition'. Hay tended to avoid occasions where he would be exposed to abuse for

> when by some uncommon Accident I have been drawn into a Country-Fair, Cock-pit, Bear-garden . . . after I have got from them I have felt the Pleasure of one escaped from the Danger of a Wreck.

The great division between the behaviour of the two social classes he ascribes to breeding and education.

While he sought the company of friends from his own background, he notes that even in this tolerant gathering there were nice problems of adjustment and accommodation to his handicap. A tall friend while in animated conversation was liable to knock Hay's hat off with an elbow or would be obliged to stoop down 'as in search of a pin' while he, Hay, would strain to look up as though taking the angle of a star with a quadrant. One of Hay's fellow magistrates happened to be a very tall man and Hay arranged to have the chairman of the Bench sit between them so that the disparity in their appearance would not provoke comment by those attending the court.

He was deeply opposed to the idea that he should seek out the company of others handicapped like himself, and preferred to be part of his social world even though it involved certain stratagems to minimize his handicap. However, he recognized that his disability placed restrictions on the range of activities open to him but did not prevent him from following a career. Among the lower classes deformity prevented a man from enlisting as a soldier ('being under standard'), or a sailor ('unable to climb the rigging' or carry a chair through lack of strength). In the 'higher life' the law was impossible ('scarce be seen over the bar'), as was the Church, since the preacher would be invisible in the pulpit, but there were ways in which he could make his mark: if not an actor then a playwright; not a herald in a procession but a merchant in the exchange; not a captain on the battlefield but a strategist or a writer describing exploits beyond his power to imitate.

Hay noted that different kinds of deformity excited different kinds of responses. He saw blindness evoking pity, but his crooked back only contempt. It was important, he thought, for the deformed person to deal with this contempt and ridicule and his advice was 'bear it like a man, forgive it as a Christian and consider it as a Philosopher' and especially to take the initiative in putting people at their ease. He found the use of humour against himself defused much of the antagonism: 'Wit will give over when it sees itself outdone and so will malice when it finds no effect.'

Hay was what we might now call, though he would have hated the idea, a handicapped person who was well integrated into society. He led a busy and useful life as an MP earning for himself the description of 'first in and last out', held minor political office, married happily and handsomely, and raised a large family to whom he seems to have been devoted. His essay shows a ready sympathy for the underdog, he was horrified at the routine cruelty to children he saw around him, but had nothing to say about disability as it affected people in the lower social classes: he was no reformer, but simply described the world as it was but with gratitude for his ability to keep away from the mob, content to use his disability as a vehicle for speculation. 'Men naturally despise what appears less beautiful or useful and their pride is gratified when they see such foils to their own persons.'

Many of the points discussed by Hay have found their way into the present psychology of handicap. It is now acknowledged that disabled people's attitudes to themselves are often shaped around the manner in which their handicap was treated in early childhood. Similarly there still exists a variety of attitudes towards different kinds of disabilities. Disability still prevents or inhibits access to occupations and professions (for example some medical schools will not accept for training a person in a wheelchair, while others will do so since there is a valuable role such a doctor could perform in, say, a group practice). Modern studies have looked at the minutiae of social interactions between normal and disabled people which Hay wrote about with irony.

But the interest in Hay's account is the light it sheds on the beginnings of a more rational, gentler acceptance of deformity, limited to a narrow segment of society, but broadening in the nineteenth century to the sentimental and philanthropic attitudes of that age.

To detail the nature and progress of these changes is beyond the scope of this book, but they include the cultivation of manners in which it was unseemly and socially inappropriate to ridicule publicly the appearance of another person; the growing scientific interest in aspects of human development, as in Itard's care and observation of the 'Wild Boy of Aveyron'; the advances in the education of the deaf, the blind and the mentally handicapped, where new techniques made communication possible; and the growth of enterprises in which the gross and grasping materialism of the time could be contrasted with a powerful philanthropic drive which, though to our eyes excessively paternalistic, nevertheless provided some haven for the disadvantaged. The nineteenth century also saw the beginnings of the involvement of central government as well as charitable organizations in the care of the handicapped, which may be symbolized by the passing of legislation at the end of the nineteenth century permitting School Boards to provide for the blind, deaf, epileptic, and mentally and physically defective children.

Two people may stand as examples of these changes in attitudes. Both stories are well known, one of long standing interest, the other more recent: they are of Helen Keller and John Merrick. If the prodigious talent of the young Mozart inclines one to despair of 'explanations' in terms of conventional theories of child development, and one is almost forced into a stumbling belief in a mystical explanation, almost as baffling is the story of Helen Keller. Anne Sullivan's remarkable efforts in transforming a child who before the age of seven was a

> 'living nullity', aware only of tactile sensations, vibrations and scents, dwelling in a world, as she wrote later that was a 'no-world', without hope, anticipation, wonder, faith or joy. For in her aimless, dayless life she was deaf, blind and unable to speak, a small animal, violent and stubborn, given to spasms of baffled rage. (Brooks, 1956: 7)

The scene in the garden at Tuscumbia where Anne makes Helen wash her drinking mug in the pump house has become part of special education's folk-lore.

> I spelled 'w-a-t-e-r' in Helen's free hand. The word coming so close to the sensation of cold water rushing over her hand seemed to startle her. She dropped the mug and stood as one transfixed. A new light came into her face. She spelled 'water' several times . . . suddenly turning round she asked for my name. I spelled 'Teacher'. (Keller, 1930: 253)

Three and a half months later she wrote in pencil:

> helen wrote anna george will given helen apple simpson will shoot bird jock will give helen stick of candy helen will give mildred medicine mother will give mildred new dress (1887)

Thirteen years later she wrote to the Chairman of the Academic Board of Ratcliffe College:

> Dear Sir,
>
> As an aid to me in determining my plans for study in the coming year, I apply to you for information as to the possibility of my taking the regular courses at Ratcliffe College.
>
> Since receiving certificate of admission to Ratcliffe last July, I have been studying with a private tutor, Horace, Aeschylus, French, German, Rhetoric, English History, English Literature and Criticism and English composition. In college I should wish to continue most, if not all of these subjects. The conditions under which I work require the presence of Miss Sullivan who has been my teacher and companion for thirteen years, as an interpreter of oral speech and as a reader of examination papers . . .

I realize that the obstacles in the way of my receiving a college education are very great – to others they may seem insurmountable; but dear Sir, a true soldier does not acknowledge defeat before the battle. (ibid.: 221)

While there are many aspects of Helen Keller's life which are of great interest, two can be selected as highly significant. The first is that she became inordinately famous, and was so from the age of ten. By 1890 a ship had been named after her, she corresponded with Oliver Wendell Holmes, was admired by Mark Twain, asked after by Queen Victoria, and received at the White House. Through the admiration of the Director of the Perkins Institution where Helen went to school, Helen was known to writers and royalty and she was described as the 'eighth wonder of the world', 'intellectual prodigy' and 'wonder girl'.

Her miraculous emergence from the silent darkness of her isolation and her prodigies of learning were so widely publicized that she became a symbol of what might be possible for a number of handicapped people, while the skilled efforts of Anne Sullivan became an inspiration to special educators everywhere. Helen Keller in herself and by her speeches and writing became a spokesperson for blind-deaf people. She had a definite view of herself as an object lesson 'showing how much can be achieved under the worst difficulties'. She believed the blind should help themselves and was against segregating them into institutions. She campaigned over the then heated problem of the different kinds of raised print for the blind, and in three years she addressed 250 public meetings to raise funds. She became a living symbol for fellow sufferers. But more importantly she knocked on the head the notion that the blind are to be pitied. She said she had never been 'corrupted by kindness', while she did not refrain from using examples of blind men and women who had made outstanding contributions, she also thought of the less exalted.

It was true, there were many instances of blind historians, economists, statesmen – mathematicians – journalists, editors – teachers – but all required a fighting spirit and a forceful personality for a blind person to succeed in these difficult professions. What was more generally called for was to teach the blind to see with their hands, as carpenters, wood-workers, weavers, chain makers. (Brooks, 1956: 96)

Helen Keller's significance is not only as a symbol of the rescue and development of an outstanding person, she was also an image of potential – perhaps hidden away in others with similar unpromising beginnings to their lives too: a splendid image made for idealists. Her other major contribution was as spokesperson for the blind and the deaf-blind. Perhaps for the first time the handicapped had an articulate champion who could command a respectful hearing on a world platform and who could demand with dignity progress without pity.

The second person I chose to represent a link between older and more contemporary attitudes to handicap is John Merrick, better known as 'The Elephant Man'. In the last few years Merrick has been the subject of a number of books, and a play and film have been made of his life.

Merrick was a concatenation of physical misfortunes.

> The most striking thing about him was his enormous mis-shapen head. From the brow there projected a huge bony mass like a loaf. While from the back of the head hung a bag of spongy, fungous-looking skin . . . the osseous growth of the forehead almost occluded one eye. The circumference of the head was no less than that of the man's waist . . . the face was no more capable of expression than a block of gnarled wood . . . the right arm was enormous size and shapeless . . . so lame he could only walk on a stick. (Drimmer, 1976: 324)

So wrote Sir Frederick Treves (1853–1923). The story of how Treves befriended John Merrick and raised money for his care is now well known. Two points from the story are relevant to us now. The first is the contrast in treatment Merrick received between his use as an object to excite vulgar curiousity as a fairground freak, and the large number of people who were helpful, kind and considerate to him. Merrick may stand for the light and the dark sides of Victorian attitudes to deformity. The second is the way in which Merrick impressed those who met him after his rescue. He was childlike in his enthusiasm, a lover of fairy stories and all tales, but what impressed his contemporaries was the survival of humanity in the face of corporeal horrors and public revulsion.

Those interested in the evolution of character might speculate on the effects of this brutish life on a sensitive and intelligent man. It would be reasonable to surmize that he would become a spiteful and malignant misanthrope, swollen with venom and filled with hatred for his fellow men or on the other hand, that he would degenerate into a despairing melancholic on the verge of idiocy. (ibid.: 333)

But he was neither of these, he was gentle, lovable, 'as amiable as a happy woman', without cynicism or resentment and apparently constitutionally incapable of uttering an unkind word.

As a spectacle of humanity Merrick was ignoble and repulsive, but the spirit of Merrick if it could be seen in the form of the living would assume the figure of an upstanding and heroic man. (ibid.: 345)

What explains Merrick's interest for us today? In part it is sociological and moral (how do we interpret Treve's motives?) and in part his appearance, even recreated on the stage, provides us with a double reassurance – a reminder of our own precious normality and the consolation that the most visually repulsive of humans contained within himself the core of what it is to be human. Hay cried out 'Is the carcass the better part of man?' No, we reply, the better part of man is affection, kindness, gentleness and freedom from revenge: this is the moral message of John Merrick. And furthermore, However much we may believe that the quintessential humanity of a man survives intact, unrevealed in his outward form, advertisers deluge our society with propaganda promoting the desirability of appropriate physical attributes: the blessings of a slim body, glossy hair, perfect teeth, clear eyes, a healthy tan, hands that are as soft as one's face, and a spotless skin. They push these notions so fervently that we might seem to be fixated on the subject, for not only are these features said to be desirable in themselves, they apparently lead to our being wanted, to our becoming successful, rich and powerful. The effect of all this is that Merrick's appearance is a confirmation of our superiority, and our delight in discovering his humanity is a sentimental sop to our conditioned revulsion, as though we half-believe the exterior man must corrupt the interior one.

Active and passive voices

Just as there are a whole range of attitudes towards disabled people so also disabled people show a variety of responses to their disability. Margaret Lester's biography (Epstein, 1968) is an account of a young woman injured in a car accident in 1960 as a result of which she was paralyzed from the chest down, and from the fracture level there was a total loss of sensation and muscular control of bodily functions. In the story of her life following the injury, she wrote of her attitudes to her disability. One of the impressive aspects is her determination to play a full and active part in family life. She describes her pleasure in her two young children and how she coped with them from her wheelchair. 'The management of babies is quite easy from a wheelchair.' Children she found accepted their 'mum in a chair' and she notes that they quickly learned to help with tasks which eased her work-load.

Running a home from a wheelchair required careful planning and she described how she did the family laundry, cooked and generally tidied up, although she had help with cleaning and dusting. She describes the adaptations to the house (such as having an abundance of low-level cupboards) to make life easier; her social life (visits to the theatre, camping), recreation (swimming) and studying (she qualified as an architect after her accident). Her account of her life as wife and mother is a valuable example of how essential roles can be sustained in spite of serious physical limitations; it also suggests a powerful propagandist voice championing a normality of life-style providing the disabled person has the right attitude: her motto was 'anything can be done', which in a sense is true, but with the attendant danger that a disabled person who does not succeed does not have the 'right attitude'. Mrs Lester places her infirmity as an objective limitation on activity but one which does not debar her from sustaining a fully normal role as wife, mother and professional.

Two years earlier, Paul Hunt had written of his experiences as someone with muscular dystrophy who had spent much of his life from the age of thirteen in a wheelchair, and in the company of others equally seriously handicapped. His perception of handicap was much darker than Margaret Lester's. He sees the disabled as occupying a special place within society and offering a challenge to many aspects of conventional relationships. 'We challenge others by being *unfortunate*, by being *useless*, by being *different*, *oppressed* and *sick*.'

By *unfortunate* he meant that the disabled person was denied access to the goods and the good things of life as these are commonly judged: occupation, marriage, children, independence of movement, etc. These possessions are 'seen as the key to entry into a promised land of civilized living' – to be without them is to be unfortunate, but even the most severely disabled people retain an ineradicable conviction that 'they are still fully human in all that is ultimately necessary'. The sight of a disabled person leading a full and rich life without the goods the rest of society thinks of as so important, sets up a strain, which is eased by explaining it away as a 'fatalistic acceptance', 'making the best of things', or a belief that in such a person we are seeing exceptional virtue (what Hunt calls the 'canonization' of the disabled). These views permit the normal to cling to their belief that disability is essentially tragic and affirms the value of the goods possessed by them.

The '*useless*' disabled is the one who has no productive capacity. Hunt realistically accepts the practical necessity of work, but queries the value that is placed on the work ethic, and suggests that the disabled are able to offer an alternative perspective for they are free from the competitive trappings that accompany work, 'we can act as a symbol for the pre-eminent claims of non-utilitarian values' and 'at the ultimate point we may only be able to suffer, to be passive through complete physical inability . . . our position gives us an extra experience of life in its passive aspects that is one half of the human reality'. A view that has a special relevance at this time.

The actual physical *differences* between able-bodied and physically handicapped people tend to mould the disabled into a distinct group through their particular experiences. Physical normality as a goal is not possible and psychological normality which would mean simply trying to be like everyone else is to be rejected. The treatment given to disabled people implies that they come to be seen rather like a member of any negatively discriminated minority group – blacks, Jews, homosexuals, and voluntary rebels like artists and prophets – so we can see the disabled as part of the subversive elements in society.

We can witness to the truth that a person's dignity does not rest even in his consciousness, and certainly that it does not rest in his beauty, age, intelligence or colour . . . Those of us with unimpaired minds but severely disabled bodies have a unique opportunity to show other people not only that our big difference from them does not lessen our worth, but also that *no* difference between men, however real, unpleasant or disturbing, does away with their right to be treated as fully human. (Hunt, 1966: 152)

Such differences are less important than those which unite men.

He sees the disabled as *oppressed* because their behaviour, personality or achievement is likely to be understood and explained by the disability. There is also the pain that comes from being at the receiving end of the over-weening superiority that some people display before the disabled. Direct cruelty he finds is uncommon but notes the existence of 'more subtle corrupting behaviour' of disregard, petty bullying, and denial of choices to which the institutionalized disabled are subjected, from the oppression of indifference to difficulties of access for wheelchair cases to public buildings and restaurants, to parental opposition to 'mixed marriages'. Disabled people as *sick* represent a condition about which we would rather not be made aware. For Hunt the disabled were living satirists, a reminder of a side of life which we prefer to ignore. Health is the new holiness and the sickness of a disabled person is tinctured with moral failure.

Hunt suggests that the position of the disabled presents a paradox. On the one hand they must strive to resist at all points any attempts to diminish them, and then, and only then, can they reach the point of 'real acceptance of what is unalterable . . . to achieve a fruitful resignation'. This latter point of view is unacceptable to some disabled people, who 'will have nothing to do with resignation as it used to be understood' (basically a view that they were lucky to be allowed to live) and in his 'fruitful resignation' there is no desire to be put out of sight and forgotten. Only when the individual's acceptance of his state is un-contaminated by unacceptable pressure to conform to a disabled role does it become possible to approach an acceptance that is constructive. Hunt's essay contains this sentence: 'The quality of the relationship the community has with its least fortunate members is a measure of its own health.' Note it is the *quality* of the relationship that is significant.

Tragic-satiric views

Attitudes to handicap are full of contradictions and ambiguities. They can be philosophic, pragmatic, charitable, positive, negative or indifferent for disability carries such a variety of valence for different people. The contrast and variety of attitudes comes from within the disabled population itself.

Two very recent examples come to mind: the first was the report on Mr James Haig, twenty-four years old and paralyzed from the neck down, who was contemplating suicide. He had detached himself from his family and his wife wanting her to lead her own life. He was reported as saying

> 'The last suicide attempt was such a mess up. But I have never changed my mind. Look at the people who have been living here for thirty or forty years', [Stoke Mandeville] he said, gazing at his silent colleagues, some eating in plastic bibs. 'I won't accept this way of life. You lose all of your dignity. Everything has to be done for you.' (*The Observer*, 31 August 1980)

(Mr Haig took his life in June 1981.)

In contrast there are disabled people who are active in wanting to change society's view of disabilities. In the same week a group called the Graeae staged a piece called 'Side Show'. The cast included among others an actor with 'no legs, just stumps which don't even reach the end of his undersized wheelchair. He is just a chest and a head, but it is a beautiful head.' The play is about a group of handicapped people in a freak show ('Does anyone here speak spastic?'). Stanley Reynolds writes: 'Here was a stage full of cripples – the only one who could walk without the aid of crutches or a stick was a young and pretty girl who was blind' (*The Guardian*, 28 August 1980). They showed that it is possible to be amusing even when making serious points as this play does about the difficulties of handicapped people in getting about, having access to public buildings and the lack of jobs; but perhaps such jokes are only permissible when delivered by those who have experienced these problems.

Our responses to handicap have certainly altered from the supernatural or demoniacal explanations favoured by the medieval mind, from the objectionable buffoonery of the Renaissance and from the sentimental stance of the nineteenth century. We have moved through phases of innocent belief in the miraculous power of science and teaching to reach out and bring forth the imprisoned mind or body from the mocking cage, to a more realistic acceptance of the possibility of disabled people leading fully normal roles, and yet there are ambiguities and uncertainties in our attitudes towards disablement and disabled people, and some of these conflicts are shared by the disabled themselves.

Finkelstein (1980) has argued that attitudes to disabled people have passed through three phases. The first was one where disablement was associated with low social status and in which blame for misfortune was attributed either to the individual or to the neglect of society. Phase two was coincidental with large-scale industrial growth which was paralleled by the development of segregated institutions for disabled people who were perceived as passive and in need of help. This phase saw the development of skilled professional help which, through its very success, led more and more disabled people to achieve independence and to begin to question the power relativities between them and the helping professions. The third phase is fuelled by new technologies, especially microelectronics, which enable a greater measure of personal independence and at this point the question of attitudes shifts from oppression and dominance to the nature of society which 'disables' impaired people. Finkelstein suggests that research into attitudes needs to take account of the physical environment, and the environmental control systems which both impaired and able-bodied people use but which have a special relevance for those with impairments. 'By . . . attacking the environmental forces that turn the medical condition of disability into psycho-social conditions of handicap, radical changes in the situation of the disabled can result' (Finkelstein, 1980: 24). The view of disabled people derived from attitude research which has neglected the environmental factor has also paid little regard to the way that environment symbolizes an oppressive relationship between impaired people and their communities.

Summary

Attitudes are acquired reaction systems to objects, persons, groups and events. Attitudes to disabilities have undergone something of a social revolution, having changed from fear, ridicule and degradation to a more accepting mode. In tracing and illustrating some of these changes examples were given of individuals whose lives mark these changes. A contrast was presented between the positive, accepting, 'anything is possible' view and the darker perspective of the disabled being unfortunate, useless, different, oppressed and sick. The contrast continued with a comparison of disablement as a life not worth living with the determination of some disabled people to 'go public' and be active in shaping opinion about the nature of disablement and attitudes towards disabled people. It was suggested that attitudes have gone through three phases, one where the disabled person was seen as helpless; a second phase of skilled professional involvement, leading to a third phase in which a new determination by disabled people questions their role as passive recipients of help.

3
Towards a new identity?

To become disabled is to be given a new identity, to receive a passport indicating membership of a separate tribe. To be born handicapped is to have this identity assigned from the moment of discovery and diagnosis. Both involve a social learning process in which the nuances and meanings of the identity are assimilated. Those who become handicapped in adult life have to cope not only with the practical implications of impairment, but also with a host of behavioural-attitudinal adjustments. These include a heightened sensitivity to others as well as a re-appraisal of oneself. The transforming process is often accomplished in the hands of professional experts in the work of handing out new identities.

As an illustration of what this change can mean we can consider the views of Sue Faircloth:

> I developed multiple sclerosis five years ago. This column is an attempt to desegregate myself – to free myself from the stereotype that I have been forced into and inhabited ever since. I suffer the ambiguity of being socially ostracized and of being public property without the usual social privacies. I found myself on the 'abnormal' side of society, I was asked to define myself in terms of 'abnormality'. It was a very self-destructive process, a symbol of the annihilation of the self. (Faircloth, 1981: 19)

Adventitious handicap is something that 'happens to other people'; while in a measure we are prepared for the indignity of infirmity that accompanies old age, there is no anticipation of the blows of chance. Having read many accounts by people who have experienced this dramatic and traumatic change in their lives one gets a sense of the importance of understanding the nature of the event which transformed them. It forms a natural and dramatic highlight in any such story but beyond that we find the search for some explanation of 'Why me?' and the answer to that question can take a lifetime of reflection.

In many accounts the writers stress the ordinariness of their lives; the everyday activities which preceded the transforming event. Dorothy Landvater in her book *David* describes in convincing detail the moments before the telephone rings to tell her that her son has been injured in a car accident. She recalls the homely, prosaic details of a busy day, the ironing of clothes, the calming routine of domestic life broken by hearing her husband answering the telephone and saying, 'I'll call the hospital and give my permission'. In such a manner the world turns upside down.

Christopher Lethbridge is out on a picnic with friends when they decide to go swimming

> 'I'll just run down that bank,' I said to myself, carefully tucking my glasses into a shoe – I was the last one in and ran down the slope to dive straight off the bank. The edge was only a couple of feet above the water and I dived flat . . . but I sensed trouble even when flying through the air . . . there was hardly a jolt; just suddenly, everything went still and I was floating face down in the water . . . I had heard Bettie's gasp before hitting the surface as she had been sitting only five yards away. The water barely reached her knees . . . 'Where are my legs?' I asked. (Lethbridge, 1974: 17–18)

Lethbridge's book from this point on is about his life as a paraplegic. Like many other victims, he puts in the minute detail ('tucking my glasses in a shoe') as does Mr Garland Minton who describes going blind, at 9·15 pm on 17 February, 1966, on Waterloo Station while drinking a cup of tea (Minton, 1974); while Denton Welch recalls cycling along a Surrey road keeping close to the curb with a long straight stretch of road ahead, although for him the road ahead was to be anything but straight (Welch, 1964). Hannah Wright (1978) started losing her sight just two days before she was due to prepare a dinner for the Westminster Medical School and on the evening of the dinner she could just see out of the corner of her eye but carried on and prepared Normandy prawns and tomato soup, terrine of hare, chicken breasts with mushrooms, hazelnut and orange ice-cream and almond biscuits for forty-three guests. These details are the precious remnants of a former intact life and identity.

For those handicapped from childhood there is usually in their stories some critical incident which informs them they are seen as significantly different. While in retrospect the crisis event which precipitated the disability is a cause for reflection, the period of initial reaction is one which leaves a permanently recallable memory.

Mr Jack Ashley's book *Journey into Silence* has on its dust-jacket 'Jack Ashley, MP' and this sums up his story. His hearing impediment has not lessened his enthusiasm for political life. In the middle of a distinguished political career, which was confidently expected to culminate in cabinet office, he underwent a comparatively routine operation which left him without effective hearing. He resigned his post as parliamentary private secretary to Mr Michael Stewart and began a strenuous programme of learning to lip-read before returning to the House.

Although I was virtually totally deaf, my other faculties were unimpaired but I did not know whether I should be able to use them effectively in Parliament. After Easter 1968, the final decision could no longer be delayed . . . The day I returned Tuesday, April 23rd, was one of the most testing and memorable of my life. In the past few months I had been fighting to preserve my political career which hung precariously by the most slender and delicate thread. If I succeeded, all the work, concentration, eye-strain [brought on by lip-reading training] and weariness would have been worthwhile. I left for the Commons exhausted, bewildered and apprehensive – but oddly hopeful. . . .

As I walked through the Members' Lobby I was aware of curious eyes observing me. There was a warm welcome from many of my friends who looked at the hearing aid, with its long cord, obviously wondering how I would manage . . . I sat down . . . Would I be able to understand the debate? I turned the powerful hearing aid to full volume . . . I could follow very little indeed. . . .

I left the chamber, took a long, deep breath, and walked into the bar. It was the most embarrassing experience of my life. Three or four members converged on me at once, shaking hands, slapping my back and welcoming my return. Others waved, and somebody handed me a glass of beer. After the affabilities someone asked me a question. I could neither hear nor lip-read him so I asked him to repeat it. He willingly repeated it but I still could not undetstand him. I asked him to repeat it again. Then I saw an expression that was to haunt me endlessly in the years ahead. It was one of total perplexity and embarrassment – he did not know how to deal with the situation . . . When he repeated the question again he was probably shouting because out of the corner of my eye I could see nearly everyone in the room turn to watch us. . . . Swift and meaningful glances were exchanged and by this time I was perspiring. I muttered apologies and hurriedly tried to finish the glass of beer . . . smiled all round, thanked them and walked out. . . .

I felt a chill and deeper sadness, as if a part of me was dead . . . My last support, that vague buzz of sound which had come to mean so much, had vanished – perhaps obliterated by the last desperate use of the hearing aid . . . I had begun a lifetime of tomb-like silence. (Ashley, 1973: 19–21)

As well as reminding us of the cruel nature of this type of handicap, Ashley's narrative points to another phase in the transformation process. This phase is a limbo, a lacuna in which the person believes that with effort and luck and a little help, he will be much as he was before. During this period there is a survival of faith that no gulf has been crossed which cannot be re-crossed. In Ashley's story we find his first attempt to hear with an aid brutally shattered that hope.

In much the same way Minton tells of a similar survival of optimism in this early period.

Ignorant of what happens to people who go blind, even though I have become one of them, I know nothing about blind people. I may be resigned to the idea of being blind but I am not yet comfortable with it. Unsure of myself I'm afraid to weigh myself in the balance . . . logically there is nothing to prevent me from mastering my disability save fear, my own fear and the fear of other people for me . . . a small part of me still hopes that this is a nightmare from which I will awake. (Minton, 1974: 22–3)

Like Ashley, Minton decided that his handicap was not going to prevent him from leading a near normal life. From the beginning he decided that he was going to hang on to his independence – independence of behaviour, attitudes and thoughts – to be most resistant to being moulded into the role of a dependent blind man. At the convalescent home his self-chosen task was 'to preserve my freedom without getting a reputation for touchiness' and he decided to go for a walk from the convalescent home to a nearby village. Up to this time his excursions had been limited to explorations of the ward in the hospital. The village was three miles away. Cane in hand he makes his way and initially all goes well. Using a path and hedge as cues he makes good progress, then

I find myself on the edge of an abyss. My heart is in my mouth. My mouth dries and I strain to see with my useless eyes. Like a child's fear of the dark my fear is unreasonable, unreasoning, but very real. . . . From now on every pace will be a self-conscious act. As a blind man I have discovered that when I am out in the street I can afford to be neither careless nor carefree. Instincts that used to be triggered off by visual stimuli are dormant now. In the fullness of time I may perhaps respond instinctively to messages sent to my brain by my fingers. Until that happens there is no instantaneous information for me. As yet my sense of touch is unpractised and it may take some time for me to adjust to the idea that objects in my path can be stars at midnight to give me bearings. (Minton, 1974: 54)

He crosses the road not knowing how to signal to traffic. Sudden noises alarm him – a dog barking, a car braking produce a strong emotional reaction for there is no visual anticipation of these sounds, his stick supplying slow and impoverished data for guidance. Eventually he feels a smooth expanse of glass – a shop window. An excited voice yells out

'Look out: you're going into that window.' Simultaneously a vice fastens on my wrists, jerking my arms up and the stick off the ground. My heart hammers against my chest. Inwardly I curse the interruption but with a supreme effort I manage to speak calmly. 'No, it's quite all right, thank you, I know where I'm going' . . . he pays no attention to my words. 'But you were going into the window.' For my already shredded nerves this was too much. Anger explodes in me. I shout back, 'No, I wasn't going into the window. I was looking for what was there and found it. I'm not mentally deficient, you know: only blind.' (ibid.: 57)

Shortly afterwards he is gently helped across the road and seeks refuge in a pub.

A female voice says, 'It's all right, sir. There's nothing in your way. Come straight forward.' Inside the bar it is blessedly quiet . . . I want to be alone. Reaching the counter I order a beer. She draws it and then comes round to the counter and leads me to a table. When I am seated she puts the glass in my hand. I take a long pull at the beer, drinking about a third of it. (ibid.: 59)

He takes a taxi back to the convalescent home.

Although with vastly different problems to face, each had to learn to deal with a completely new set of attitudes, to other people ('the complexity of embarrassment') and to oneself, and with the necessity of constant vigilance where 'every pace [was] a conscious act'. Neither had yet appreciated fully the true limits of their handicap nor yet the full possibilities that existed.

Out on a limb

Less overwhelming than blindness and deafness, the loss of a hand or an arm still represents a trauma. G.W. Beattie recounts what happened to his wife following an accident. She found a host of apparently simple tasks impossible – tying shoes, eating, unscrewing a jar; that her appearance had changed for 'coats and dresses hang at odd angles'. She had to deal with looks and stares, becoming 'stigmatized like a slave with a brand'. Everyday language contains its traps – 'can I give you a hand?'. 'Your status changes and with it go the privileges of independent action, and even the assumption of soundness of mind. You become a member of a recognizably different breed' (Beattie, 1979: 510). For the amputee the new artificial arm requires a body-machine integration but it is also a sign, like the long cane or the hearing aid, by which you can be identified. Beattie describes a visit to the Artificial Limb and Appliance Centre:

Time to meet the doctor (and his technician). The doctor seems a bit embarrassed. This is reflected in his language which immediately becomes metaphorical and technical . . . His language also shifts very quickly into the third person. He refers to my wife as 'she'. Communication begins to be directed via me, despite the fact that I am sitting a long way off. (ibid.: 510)

They are shown a box of artificial arms and a coloured catalogue and have to choose a mechanical arm complete with a hook and capable of being fitted with several devices which would enable Mrs Beattie to type, knit, sew, darn and drive a car (none of which she chose to do before the accident). Later the 'cosmetic' arm was produced — functionally useless but more natural looking.

Only much later did he produce the cosmetic arm. Yet my wife's first response to the accident was not to express concern about her ability to pick up pencils, but to worry if she would still be able to go on a beach in a bikini. Three weeks after the accident appearance and disguise are her main concerns. Appearance is only a trivial matter when you fall within the bounds of what is acceptable. (ibid.: 511)

David Fishlock in *Man Modified* (1969) devotes a chapter to the achievements of medicine, engineering and electronics in developing new technologies for sick and disabled people. Amongst the descriptions of powered limbs, artificial larynxes, pacemakers and dialysis machines he devotes a section to 'spinal man' with an account of practices which enable paraplegics to return to 'a surprisingly normal domestic and workaday life after an average span of twenty weeks in hospital' (p. 106) and quotes medical opinion that the extent of recovery is no longer the severity of the spinal injury, but is mainly governed by the personality and attitude of the patient. The interface between people and machinery is nowhere more subtle and complex than where the machine replicates a part of the body which is 'visible'. As Beattie points out, rehabilitation restores former 'capacities, rank, reputation and so on' and artificial limbs are not judged by users only on the grounds of functional effectiveness but also on the manner in which the prosthetic device protects their image of themselves — if not *homo intactus* then at least *homo disguisus*.

So far in this chapter we have looked at selected aspects of the process of people being transformed and given a new social identity. The examples chosen are from those disabilities – spinal injury, sensory loss and amputation – which are morally blameless. A different picture seems to emerge with another kind of transforming event: epilepsy. Epilepsy differs from other handicaps in two significant ways. It is less obvious and might be regarded as an episodic handicap with the person between seizures 'presenting' in a normal manner. It is also a condition which still attracts to its possessor a measure of social ostracism.

Epilepsy, as the British Epilepsy Association describes it, is 'a brief disruption in the normal activity of the brain. It can affect people of all ages, backgrounds and levels of intelligence. It is not a disease, or an illness.' Some injuries may be of the *grand mal* (often preceded by a cry, a sudden fall and convulsive movements), *psychomotor attack* (patient is conscious but may not be able to speak), *minor motor seizure*, and *absence* or *petit mal* (momentary clouding of consciousness). Margiad Evans (1978) describes these attacks:

> It caused no pain, it lasted a few seconds, I saw and heard and moved while it happened. I have often crossed a room, and, while not losing sight or bearings, not known *how* I crossed it. The sequence of consciousness was so little broken by it that after it had happened it seemed not an atom of time or myself had been missing, and I only knew it had happened by the numbing sensation in the centre of the brain which followed it.
> . . .
> When it happened to me while crossing a room I have, if I may so illustrate it, left myself on one side and come to myself on the other, while feeling an atom of time divided the two selves, and the room might divide the figures of myself, supposing anyone could create two figures of me . . . I was afraid of there being . . . a real split in me. It took me a whole year of suffering and possibly a dozen major fits, to disentangle myself from the terror of mental disorder. Has not every one of us a mental image of himself which he watches ceaselessly, which he must watch, and which for his health's sake and sanity's sake, deviates from the self seen by everyone else?
> (Evans, 1978: 39–40)

If the transformation process for handicaps like blindness or paralysis is made by some interaction between the person, his handicap and the attitudes of other people to him, in epilepsy the shaping process is highly dependent on the cues, advice and reactions of other people. Sue Cooke in *Ragged Owlet* (1979) describes how one day she was in the library at school and 'the next thing I knew I was lying on the carpet in a dreamy haze . . . In between this unlikely dream that I was actually lying flat on my back during a school lesson, there were phases of complete oblivion and I had no idea what had actually occurred' (p. 9). Two days later she appeared before the Head of the school who after some preamble said: 'You understand that your life will undergo a major change now. You cannot look on matters as you used to. You are different now and always will be different.' Only gradually over a period of fifteen months did she begin to understand the label that had been pinned on her.

The label 'epilepsy' carries with it so many disadvantages that it is a powerful motive to encourage 'passing' as normal. This may be seen in linguistic strategies as when people refer to their seizures as 'fainting fits' or 'black-outs'. There are legal limitations on certain occupations, such as heavy goods or passenger vehicle driving (an epileptic may drive a private vehicle though sometimes he or she has to pay an added insurance premium) and teaching physical education, and such restrictions may encourage concealment. Social attitudes towards epilepsy and epileptics are a more serious barrier than legal ones, for the epileptic is seen as tainted, and moreover has a transmissible taint. (There may be a genetic component, but the genetically-associated condition only accounts for a small proportion of those with epilepsy.) Some parents have commented that the physical management of a child with epilepsy is less of a problem than the psychological damage associated with rejection by the child's peers (Epilepsy Congress, 1977). It seems that epilepsy evokes fear in both the epileptic and in those around him. *Epilepsy News* (1978) published a letter by a woman who was concerned about her daughter who at seventeen had to fill in an application form for a job in one of the public services:

Question: Do you have epilepsy? Answer: No. Does any member of your family have epilepsy or *any other mental illness*? And I, who had always taught my children to tell the truth, counselled my daughter to say NO. Whether I was right to do so I shall never know but I couldn't bear to think that she might be refused admission to her chosen career because of an idiosyncrasy of mine.

As Sue Cooke points out it takes time even for well-counselled people with epilepsy to shake off the fear and superstition that epilepsy is a mental illness. 'The tradition of believing fits to be a sign of mental illness is so strong that many of us, even faced with neurological facts, still feel the unfairness of stigma' (p. 29); as far as employers are concerned 'epileptic' was on par with 'loony' (p. 50).

The handicapped role

Edwin Thomas (1970) argues that whether handicapped from birth or in later life the disabled person 'has some segment of his behaviour repertoire that is different from his normal fellow humans'. He describes several of the roles which are related to disability, among which is the 'disabled patient'. Two aspects of this role are selected by Thomas for special emphasis: the 'sick role' and the 'hospital role'. With the onset of impairment the individual is cast into the role of a sick person and according to Parsons (1951) this involves a measure of exemption from normal roles (if you are not well you cannot be expected to go to work). Recovery is either through spontaneous remission or by placing himself in the hands of those who can make him better, and since being sick is socially defined as undesirable, it is regarded as a temporary state. To be sick is to be defined as in need of help and the role obligation is a requirement to co-operate with those offering help. Since disability is often associated with hospitalization, Thomas also draws upon sociological studies which have identified the following aspects of hospital expectation. First there is the generalized expectation of dependency, marked out by obedience to rules and norms of the hospital, and in which the adult surrenders most of the decisions about his life to those in charge (the compliant patient is good). As in the sick role the patient must give up his normal roles and is encouraged to forget about his life outside the hospital and focus on getting well.

Secondly the patient is expected to give up most claims to status and prestige which he had outside the hospital and his status within the hospital is dependent upon his moral character as a patient, his chances of recovery, and even perhaps upon the rarity of his complaint. It is a further expectation that suffering and pain are part of being ill and should 'be borne with as much grace as possible', and that treatment often involves pain. How the patient handles pain will be part of his moral character as a patient. Finally the patient must learn to live with a measure of diagnostic uncertainty in which either the hospital staff do not know what is wrong or if they do are uncertain as to the best course of treatment or may choose to deny the patient access to the real diagnosis.

David (1964) records that, in the case of polio victims, when the diagnosis was certain, the information would be filtered as 'treatment personnel sought to cushion its impact [diagnosis] by hedging, evading questions, and acting as though the outcome was still uncertain'. Strong (1979) has shown how doctors use a lengthy time-scale in which to drip-feed droplets of information to parents of handicapped infants. This process Goffman describes as 'cooling the mark out', i.e. 'getting the patient ultimately to accept and put up with a state-of-being that is initially intolerable to him' (Thomas, 1970: 254).

To the extent that the person affected by an illness is required to undergo hospitalization, he or she will experience, as do all patients, the requirements of the sick role. An important aspect of this role is that the patient agrees with official wisdom that he *is* sick or impaired and begins to redefine himself as altered. What Thomas claims happens to disabled people is that the requirements of the sick role are made enduring. The transient nature of the role expectation of the patient who is ill and then recovers becomes permanent for disabled people. The exemption from responsibility is extended, diagnostic uncertainty prolonged, as are the requirement to endure pain and the struggle to get well. This latter point is modified in the case of disabled people to mean a striving to make the most of surviving capacities and *motivation* becomes the key rehabilitation concept, which can be a positive re-building concept or another burden. The man who wants to die rather than live in a wheelchair, simply has not grasped the role requirements; he is still looking at his disability as though he were normal, whereas he should be accepting his disability and using his surviving faculties!

It should be noted that this description of the disabled role carries a potential danger since it tends to over-generalize certain aspects of social behaviour. But something like the role model seems to exist as we saw in the quotation from Sue Faircloth at the beginning of this chapter. The role prescription is to be regarded as a negative model − one to be shunned − for the task of the person who is disabled and for his or her professional helpers is to avoid casting him into such a role. The central task is to reconstruct the pre-trauma identity as minimally changed as counselling and technology can achieve.

Denton Welch, in his beautifully written book *A Voice Through a Cloud* (1966) helps us see this aspect of the handicapped role not as sociological abstraction, but as human experience. Following his accident he is taken to hospital where he tries to talk to the nurses to get some answers to the questions running through his mind, to make some point of human contact in a world suddenly a compound of fear and pain.

> 'Now just you keep still. We don't want any more of that talking' . . . They told me not to be silly and make a fuss. All the time they were watching me and judging me. They were not taking anything I said seriously. 'Stop it,' the nurses said together. 'You'll wake the others': 'Just show me what you're made of instead of creating. You are naughty . . . we do all this work for you and this is your return.' (Welch, 1966: 14–27)

Welch also shows the kindly more natural side of hospital life and noted the action of the nurse who brought him some hot milk. 'While she was away I thought she must be a very new nurse: she had not yet learned to become inhuman but was trying to learn the trick.' For the nurses the patient is cared for by all the scrupulous requirements of professional standards, but in return the patient must abide by the rules of his new role with its expectation of conformity. Welch goes on to describe his feelings: the poison of fear, the sharp knife of pain, and the even deeper pain of a lost identity with as yet no new one to take its place.

> I tried to lull myself to sleep . . . but all the pleasant things that only yesterday I liked so much rose up to haunt me. I think of

eating delicious food, wearing good clothes, feeling proud and gay, going for walks, singing and dancing alone, fencing and swimming and painting pictures with other people, reading books. And everything seemed horrible and thin and nasty as soiled paper. I wondered how I could ever have believed in these things, how I could even for a moment have thought they were real. Now I knew nothing but real pain, heat, blood, tingling loneliness and sweat. I began to almost gloat on the horror of my situation and surroundings. I felt paid out, dragged down, punished finally. Never again would my own good fortune make me feel guilty. I could look at any beggar, or blind people in the face now. Everything I had loved was disgusting: and I was disgusting too. (ibid.: 25)

The transforming process and its experience is seldom without an element of stress. Role stress occurs when opposing and irreconcilable expectations are held about behaviour. These opposing expectations may be held by the person as it were at war within himself, or between himself and others. We may imagine that both kinds of stress are experienced by the disabled person in the transformation period. Welch's brief confrontation with the nurses was an attempt to assert the survival of an undamaged personality and wholeness of spirit struggling to avoid the imposition of a sick role, but within himself there is another battle in which the claims for normality vie with a perception of self which, at that moment, is seen as non-normal. As Thomas pointed out, role conflicts are likely to exist as the newly disabled person fluctuates in his beliefs about himself. Others around him may have views about his condition which clash with his private view of himself. Further the disabled person has to manage alternating perceptions of his status and capacities: in one situation he might be regarded as helpless and in another be asked to be determined and self-sufficient. From the perspective of role theory the transformed person has to adapt to a new set of role requirements. He will experience an uncomfortable discontinuity between his former and his new role, will experience stress and conflict in defining his new roles and will have to accommodate an alternative image of the self (from self-reliant, autonomous and independent to dependent and others-reliant). It seems as though there is no social niche for the handicapped or at least only one which provides unambiguous guidelines. 'There simply are not uniform, clear rules for disabled persons in the same way that there are rules for the non-disabled person' (Thomas, 1970: 269). A compounding factor is lack of knowledge among lay people about the nature and psychological sequel of impairment which of course does not prevent the existence of stereotypic beliefs.

> This lack of tradition, consensus and knowledge surrounding the social niche of the disabled has a singular consequence: the customary social moorings that control the choice of behaviour in human encounters are weakened. The disabled and those who behave towards them consequently have more choices of behavioural alternatives. Speaking more generally, there is *role optionality* . . . The society and culture also shape the choice of options, directing them . . . towards normalization. . . . The society is created and run for the benefit of the normal. (Thomas, 1970: 269–71)

Those in the middle of the transforming period have within them these values towards normality and disability, and must face the emotional and social implications of these held values as they apply to the self.

In this brief account of some of the features associated with the changes in identity which can accompany sudden impairment or disablement the focus has been on individual and personal reactions. Such transformations are seldom without implications for roles and relationships. As significant as the changes which may take place within a person are the changes to long-established roles and strategic relationships. Disablement can mean modification to personally significant roles such as mother, breadwinner or friend. Modification to these roles may be the result of functional impairment or perception that the effective performance of such roles is the prerogative of the able-bodied. Whether transformation occurs in self-image and/or role, we find in the accounts of many who have experienced this period of change the discovery of dormant reserves of physical and psychic energy which enable them to move through the transformation period into a period of adjustment and accommodation. For the lucky ones similar unsuspected reserves are found in those around them who are important in their lives. In the process of transformation there is often the discovery of greater sensitivity, a sharpening of perception, a finer appreciation of what is truly valued and what is trivial, but psychologically what is of maximal importance is that at the end of the process should be the survival of the self, in essence unchanged.

Summary

Sudden loss of previously intact functional capacities was selected as a clear example of one of the changes in identity which can follow impairment. In many autobiographies the critical precipitating event and immediate prior circumstances assume the status of a marker in the life of that person. Such events and their detailed description are more than a dramatic device, for through this mechanism the pre-trauma personality is established and the transformation process an interlude after which the former self re-emerges, modified but not mutilated. During the transformation period there are episodes of profound depression and periods of optimism that former capacities and roles may be recovered undamaged, which were stages in the adjustment process where a level of accommodation could be reached in which the new data − the impairment and its consequences − could be integrated into a new style of living. Some of the negative aspects of the disabled role were discussed with the assumptions of lowered capacities to perform customary social roles. It was noted that the process of transformation was often accompanied by the discovery of unsuspected reserves of determination and skill which could be brought to the task of a changed life-style.

4
Interactions

Social psychologists believe, and for once common sense supports them, that there is a tendency for people to form complex impressions of others on the basis of quite limited information. (I overheard a colleague saying of a post-graduate student, 'I knew he was a Trotskyite by his shirt.') While we are aware that our initial impressions may be in error, co-operative subjects are willing to express opinions about others, on the basis of photographs, as to their intelligence, race, religion, educational level, warmth, likeability and honesty. There is also a tendency to evaluate others in a consistent or global manner so that the impression the other person makes on us is seen as forming a coherent totality. Favourable or unfavourable impressions formed in one context often extend to other contexts, and as we are also liable to project on to others our own characteristics so we are much more accurate in rating others whom we see as 'like us' than people who are obviously different. Instant impression-formation will be a factor in shaping how two people initially relate to one another.

In the last decade researchers have become fascinated with the details of how we interact. These details include spoken words, their rate and intonation, facial expressions, eye-to-eye contacts and avoidances, bodily posture, how near or how far away we stand from each other, and the gestures that accompany communication. From these minutiae we get the feeling that each encounter is a coded performance which has to be translated and that on the whole we become competent decoders of both the obvious and hidden meanings contained within the interactional messages. As individuals we never meet the sociological abstraction 'society', what we do encounter are other people and it is through such meetings we build an image of our society, how to relate to it and where we stand within it.

It might seem to be a little unfair to assert the possibility that physical appearance is a key determinant of how people respond to us, after all there is only a limited amount of impression-management possible in this area. Paper and pencil tests show that people do not rate physical appearance as very important in their liking of other people; however their behaviour suggests otherwise. In one experiment couples were assigned to each other at a dance on a random basis and questionnaires were given out at the end of the dance. They revealed that none of the measures of intelligence, social skills, or personality was related to 'liking' except physical appearance. Other studies have shown that good-looking children are more popular with their peers than the less handsome, and tall people are seen as more suited for positions of leadership than short people, so the existence of physical-appearance factors in shaping (at least) initial impressions of other people are important.

Such physical-appearance factors become more significant when the physical trait is correlated with value-belief systems: colour prejudice is an obvious example of such a correlation. Something similar seems to occur with highly visible disabilities. Visible impairment provides a signal or sign to the other person which stimulates a differential reaction system. One reaction system is simply avoidance – the diverted glance or movement to prevent contact; another might be a forced 'normality'. Davis (1964), using material derived from people with visible dis-abilities, attempted a description of interactions between them and 'normals'. He found that there were stages through which interactions passed and that since the disabled did not constitute a sub-culture, imputations of deviance arose as 'genuine interac-tional emergents' rather than the product of minority-group stereotyping. That is, if there are perceived differences between the visibly handicapped and the non-handicapped, such dif-ferences are not only evoked during interactions, they are a product of interactional awkwardness.

For Davis such interactions are subject to uncertainty and a degree of experimentation in roles in the absence of clearly established rules of conduct. Encounters become exploratory and investigative, and there is no instant recipe. He suggests that the handicap becomes a threat to sociability for four main reasons:
1 The handicap tends to become the focal point of the interac-

tion. In ordinary encounters a measure of diffuseness of attention is regarded as necessary, and the orientation is towards the whole person, whereas in encounters with the visibly disabled there is the issue of the perceptual magnet of the visible handicap influencing the desirable social behaviour, to feign it has not been noticed.

2 The question of the appropriate type and amount of emotional display that is 'right' for such encounters: enthusiastic ('*Delighted* to meet you') or soberly grave?

3 Contradiction of attributes: the inexperienced normal sometimes finds it hard to create a wholeness or totality of impression if there is an apparent contradiction between the disabled's attributes, as say, between appearance and intelligence, occupation and interest. 'Sociable interaction is made more difficult as a result because many normals can only resolve the seeming incongruities by assimilating or subsuming (often in a patronizing or condescending way) the other attribute to the handicap.'

4 Doubts and uncertainty about the extent to which the handicapped person can participate in social activities (and he quotes the example of someone meeting a blind person at a party after which some of the party are going to the theatre. Does one include him in the invitation?). These then are some of the factors which present a measure of strain in social encounters.

In his analysis of social encounters Davis describes such encounters as passing through three stages; fictional acceptance, 'breaking through' and normal relationships:

the overture phases of a sociable encounter are to a degree regulated by highly elastic fictions of equality and normality. In meeting those with whom we are neither close nor familiar manners dictate that we refrain from remarking on or otherwise reacting too obviously to those aspects of the person which in the privacy of our thoughts betoken important differences between ourselves and others. . . .

The visibly handicapped is customarily recorded . . . the surface acceptance . . . like the poor man at the wedding, . . . sufficient that he is here, he should not expect to dance with the bride. (Davis, 1964: 127)

Here the problem for the visibly disabled is to allow this polite fiction to proceed so that later on he may disavow any imputation of deviance, but if the relationship is to develop, this fictional normality must end. It ends when either person allows the fact of the disability to enter the relationship in a non-stigmatizing way, such as in the use of 'taboo' words by both parties. At the third stage there is acceptance of normality and equality of status and only then does it become possible to admit to the encounter some of the genuine restraints which impairment imposes. This, writes Davis, is a tricky operation for the disabled person integrating a major claim to normality while simultaneously offering minor disclaimers.

Experimental evidence

That visibly handicapped people and 'normals' experience some awkwardness in relating to one another has been further illustrated by controlled experiments and careful observation. Robert Kleck (1968) took the view that visible handicap is a stigma which is discrediting to its possessor and this stigma spreads to those in close contact with the handicapped person, which leads to the avoidance of contacts of a long-term nature. However, it was noted that when subjects are asked to give their impression of both a disabled and non-disabled person, they consistently report more favourable impressions of the former. In one experiment the subject and the experimenter's confederate exchanged information concerning certain attitudes and each subject met one of the confederates on two occasions where the confederates presented as himself (normal) or in a wheelchair. The interactions were filmed and analysed and appeared to show that in 'disabled'-normal encounters eye-to-eye contact is similar to that in normal-normal encounters, but subjects in the 'disabled'-normal situation showed 'greater motoric inhibition' (the subjects were more controlled and careful in their movements), demonstrated a much more positive impression of the 'disabled' confederate, concealed their views and expressed opinions which they felt were consistent with those they assumed were held by the 'disabled' person.

The similarities in the frequency of eye-to-eye contact in both 'disabled' and normal settings may be explained by the importance of the face as a source of information being strong enough to overcome any tendency for gaze-avoidance. The motoric inhibition suggests that subjects were under some stress, being uncertain how to behave 'naturally'. The highly favourable impression formed of the 'disabled' confederate may be due to initial expectation of a low level of functioning which was discomforted during the interview and which in turn gave rise to a super-normal evaluation. Subjects stated their views on the significance of sport and they were much less enthusiastic when talking to the 'disabled' confederate. Kleck concluded that this study showed that in initial encounters the disabled are experiencing a qualitatively different interaction pattern (from normal-normal patterns) and may be receiving information and attitudes which are significantly modified to meet their perceived needs.

As well as conducting highly controlled experiments social psychologists have reported on experiments of a more naturalistic nature. It was noted earlier that one of the facets of non-verbal behaviour was the distance between interacting people in different kinds of social situations. Social distance is fluid and shifts with the nature of social requirements. Hall used the term 'proxemics' and measured these distances in terms of intimate, personal, social and public occasions and showed that the social distances we use are well understood and carefully monitored. It is as though we carry around with us a flexible territorial boundary adjusting its shape and area according to the demands of the moment and our feelings towards the other person. Worthington (1977) decided to look at the problem of whether different kinds of social distances are used between normal-handicapped interactions and normal-normal interactions. She speculated that the disabled as a stigmatized class carried with them a zone of contamination and that normal subjects would seek to remain on the periphery of this zone and to reduce the time spent within or near the zone. The use of closer contact and extended time would show the absence of this effect and the working of empathy or pro-social behaviour.

Using the lounge of an airport, the confederate sat in a lobby with a street map on his lap. He asked people for directions to a certain freeway. The point of nearest approach was recorded (the floor had been marked at distances of $1\frac{1}{2}$, $2\frac{1}{2}$, 4, 7 and 12 feet corresponding to Hall's data on personal and social distances) as was the time spent by the person giving the information. The procedure was repeated, but this time the confederate posed as a disabled person seated in a wheelchair. There were twenty-nine people in the control situation (normal) and thirty-four in the experimental one (disabled). The data showed statistically significant differences in the mean approach distances with a greater mean difference operating in favour of the experimental mode. However, there were no differences in the amount of time spent in giving information in the two settings.

Worthington concluded that these data provided confirmation of the contamination view since the amount of personal space was greater in the disabled condition but equally there was no lessening of the desire to help. But they 'did not want to catch whatever it was the stigmatized experimenter had'. Interestingly, two subjects displayed behaviour which contrasted with the behaviour of subjects in general: one approached the disabled experimenter at a intimate distance and the other showed unusually helpful behaviour. They were a black male and a Caucasian female.

The passive view

The analysis of Davis and the experimental methods of Kleck and Worthington may be flawed in one important respect. They all appear seriously to overestimate the passivity of the disabled person in social encounters. The underlying theme is that the disabled person is essentially reactive to the behaviour of others (others take the lead and he or she follows). There is little room in this type of work for acknowledging the skill of some disabled people in taking a positive lead in interactions, and almost no mention that disabled people are often extremely perceptive about others' feelings and reactions; they can be accomplished in making relationships work smoothly. The conclusion that might be drawn from research is that disabled people perpetually encounter others who are embarrassed and awkward, who seek to camouflage their true views and who perceive disabled people as possessing qualities that are admirable. That this does occur is not deniable, but as an image of interaction it neglects the disabled person as a skilled co-manager of interactions and also neglects the vitally important point that the majority of our *significant* relationships are not of the casual, ephemeral kind, but are with people with whom intimacy, friendship and trust are built up over time. Disabled people have a wealth of experience to bring to new relationships and while we can be uneasy at a first meeting, our greatest allies will be disabled people themselves who appreciate our feelings and can help us through any awkward phase. My impression is that many disabled people have a heightened awareness of the nuances of social behaviour and are quick to spot and ease embarrassment, and equally are adept at distinguishing an honest but clumsy attempt at friendship from one that is fraudulent. It is perception of the awkwardness of initial encounters that renders non-involvement an attractive option. Not so long ago I visited a rehabilitation centre where I met a young man who had been badly injured in a road accident. 'This is James,' said the supervisor, 'one of our new members.' James looked at me from his wheelchair, with a weighing expression. I reached out my hand and he offered me his. The hand, which had been under a blanket, was covered in metalic strips to which the fingers and thumb were fastened. The metal claw and my hand paused about an inch apart. Then he put his metal claw into mine. The metal was warm from his skin. He looked at me again and grinned.

Special problems

It has often been suggested that certain kinds of disabilities create particular problems for social behaviour. Lukoff (1972) argued that blindness evokes a particular set of attitudes, among which are found compassion, sentimentality and the attribution of favourable characteristics. Part of this 'appeal' may stem from the apparent ease with which it is possible for the sighted person to comprehend how pre-eminent among our senses is vision. Another element in the positive attitude to blindness is that while comprehensible, blindness does not distort the total body-image and leaves intact major areas of behaviour, especially language. Although it has been suggested that interactions with blind people can present minor problems (such as the absence of conventional non-verbal accompaniments of speech, e.g. appropriate facial expressions) these are counter-balanced by skills in using other forms of feedback. The principal interactional difficulties of the blind appear to stem from the pervasive attitudes to their handicap, tempting a reflection on the problems of over-positive attitudes.

Deafness presents a different picture. The absence of standard visual signs of impediment suggest a normal body image which does not convey anticipatory information to others in the way a wheelchair and long cane do, so anticipatory and avoidance mechanisms are not alerted, and the impediment intrudes unexpectedly into the interactional context. Difficulties in recept-ive or expressive language are greater constraints on interactional smoothness than lack of vision or visible handicaps. Stress in such encounters is likely to encourage brief and stylized relationships. If the characteristic affective colouring of interactions with the blind is compassion, with the deaf it is irritation. This irritation is at its root provoked by the failure to communicate with another person which becomes displaced on to that person. There is also the threat which a deaf person poses to our conventional repertoire of social skills. For example, we learn through experience that there are appropriate rate, pitch and volume of speech for each social occasion, and to find oneself shouting where we would normally use a lower volume is exhausting and irritating especially if we are attempting to convey the impression that we are *not* shouting but talking normally. Another cause of awkwardness is that the normal hearer-speaker has difficulty in knowing what level of voice production is acceptable to the hard of hearing; nor is it always possible to gauge with accuracy the degree of lip-reading skill possessed by the deaf person, nor the quality of our own lips as shapers of words. The communication problem for the deaf person is equally intense: he or she may have to focus intently and with considerable effort on the other person's lips, putting together the 'heard' parts with what was not clearly registered to make sense of the utterance. Face-to-face communication is obviously best and it is extremely difficult for a deaf person to lip-read while walking alongside another, and there is the indignity of being addressed through an interpreter.

The significance of the face as a source of information has been emphasized by social psychologists and its central role in shaping interactions is dramatized in the case of those with facial disfigurements. A recent television programme on the work of the surgeon Archibald McIndoe and his wartime aircrews, many of whom suffered extreme facial disfigurement, brought this reaction from one critic:

There was no blinking the fact that some of the visages on show still looked fairly rugged. Lipless mouths, tacked on noses, stub ears. But one of the several heartening things about the programme was the way the personalities came shining through the damage. You found yourself getting used to it. Easy for us, of course: we aren't exactly obliged to wear the face. (James, *The Observer*, 10 June 1979)

Wearing the face is exactly what Doreen Trust has been doing all her life. Born with one of those purple birth marks across her left cheek she has written in *Skin Deep* (1978) of her childhood experiences and her later work in Skin Camouflage and Disfigurement Therapy. During her early years she was shunned by other children and made many attempts to mask her blemish. Even today after running a successful therapy service she has to 'count ten before entering a crowded room'. She knows of parents who seek skin camouflage for their facially disfigured children, but while understanding this wish believes there is a danger of children learning to hide behind the make-up and coming to believe there is something wrong with themselves. She has found that disfigurements are seen as strange and threatening, patients get so concerned about their appearance that they cannot be seen by anyone, not even husband or wife, without make-up. A compelling paradox: your disfigurement makes you and others uncomfortable so you cover it up; covering it up makes you unable to confront (face?) your face.

What is thought to be the most painful aspect of epilepsy is the 'stigma of the disorder and the attitudes of others towards those afflicted'. Harrison and West (1977) conducted a survey of public images of epilepsy and found in their sample people who had known someone with epilepsy and others who had never met such a person. Both groups expressed 'negative' views about epileptics (violent, aggressive types, timid and withdrawn, highly strung, retarded, nervy, 'mental', sluggish and antisocial).

Negative images were not the perogative of those with

experience. Respondents who had not known an epileptic were equally likely to attribute 'deviant' characteristics. But the most important finding is that contact with sufferers seems to confirm and generate 'negative' stereotypes. (Harrison and West, 1977: 282)

The researchers conclude that public images of epilepsy are part manufactured since the public is shielded from those with the most serious problems, only meeting those with less incapacitating problems or those who are unlikely to disclose their status, leaving opinion or prejudice unchanged. Of interest was their suggestion that exhortation would not be very effective in changing attitudes, but that attitudes would change if more people with epilepsy 'like other groups subject to prejudice would not conceal their predicament, but confront it'. Easy for us of course, we aren't obliged to fear a fit.

The social predicament

One of the interactional problems is the wish of disabled people to be perceived as socially normal (non-deviant), while simultaneously presenting limitations to that identity. By offering the self as socially conventional (having the roles, rights, responsibilities and status of the whole person) yet possessing physical limits to marginal and central aspects of that self-definition, the disabled person presents a moral and tactical conundrum. For the normal person, the interactional puzzle is how to shift his behaviour according to the requirements of the situation: to change from an interactional mode that implies normality and equality, to those where inequalities of functional effectiveness become apparent and which may be used for the benefit, comfort and aid of the disabled person without the implication that differentials in effectiveness mean loss of normality, equality and personal dignity. How do we offer assistance without implying that the other person is infantile and inferior? One way is by compartmentalizing the need for assistance and its gift into distinct and value-free areas of the interaction. The social task for the disabled is to signal that aid is needed in a manner which does not challenge his social orthodoxy and for the other to respond to the signal without ostensible hair-trigger alertness, over-anxiety or condescension and for both to compartmentalize the status-endangering aspect of their relationship as a practical necessity. Aid and assistance can be given stripped to its minimal necessary form without additional emotional coloration and this is often followed by a slight 'recovery' period after which the naturalistic level of the interaction may be resumed.

The status of beneficiary is hard to handle with dignity. The distinguished blind scholar Pierre Villey wrote that 'all causes of absolute inequality among men engender vices'. The inequality of blindness produced the vice of humiliation. For the blind person this infiltrated not only their work and professional lives, but at an everyday level too.

> The little services for which he must count on one person or another are not only a slight handicap to the blind man, they work him up to a state of worry that becomes a torture . . . His freedom of action and of speech seem to be fettered. The necessity of having a guide besides being tiresome, is also embarrassing. A stranger must read his letters, is present nearly always, and even if he should not be guilty of any indiscretion such as a susceptible imagination is apt to magnify, the very presence of this person is distressful. A thin skin is also very easily wounded by words and gestures which seem to prove to a blind man that he is confounded with an impotent or a feeble-minded person . . . what shocks a blind man is exaggerated pity or a great show of admiration, which is just as painful, and is the result of the same insulting ignorance. (Villey, 1930: 377–8)

It seems to me that one way of describing the kind of stance that would be most helpful would be to call it 'unobtrusive availability'.

Garland Minton – and we have used one example from his book to illustrate a highly charged social encounter – also gives an illustration of an initial encounter: one of unobtrusive availability. It occurred immediately after the shop window incident.

> A fresh voice breaks in . . . I am glad to hear it. Calm and quiet, not overlaid with emotion and not accompanied by clutching fingers, the calmness of her voice awakens a corresponding

calm in me. She says, 'Are you all right? I don't want to
interfere but I saw what happened and wondered if I could do
anything for you?' 'Thank you,' I reply, 'I'd be grateful if you'd
take me past these shops.' 'Shall I take your arm or will you
take mine?' 'Oh, I'll take yours. It's better for me to follow than
to lead.' Together we proceed along the pavement and by the
time we have passed the shops I have recovered my composure.
I disengage my arm, thank the woman and continue on my
way. (Minton, 1974: 58)

Minton is good at describing how boring train journeys can be for
blind people – the sounds of the wheels, the occasional remark
from fellow travellers, compounded by the special 'English'
problem of how to behave on trains – which become even more
acute when one of our fellow travellers happens to be blind.

> Every attempt at real conversation is abortive. It seems that the
> normal restraint of travellers on British Rail is reinforced by the
> presence of a blind man. Or is it just me? Am I too conscious of
> myself? Usually, I don't find it difficult to make conversation
> but for some inexplicable reason I cannot do it now. It seems
> that no one else in the carriage is on the same wavelength as me.
> (ibid.: 75)

Then he meets a travelling companion who does find it easy to
talk to him, partly because she has some appreciation of his
situation, for her own husband has lost his sight. She speaks:

> 'My husband went blind about ten years ago. It made him
> furious when people treated him as though he had lost his wits.
> So many intelligent people are quite stupid in dealing with the
> disabled. Most of all my husband disliked it when people asked
> *me* how he was. Sometimes it was embarrassing because he
> would say "Why the hell don't you ask me?"' (ibid.: 78)

And that presumably would be recorded as another instance of
the touchiness of the blind.

Ashley had some very perceptive remarks to make on the
difficulties he experienced shortly after losing his hearing: 'Life
was eerie. People appeared suddenly by my side, doors banged
noiselessly, dogs barked soundlessly and heavy traffic glided
silently passed me. Friends chattered gaily in total silence'

(Ashley, 1973: 133). Among the sharpest of losses was that of the human voice, not being able to join in casual conversation, no more repartee and no more jokes, being confined to simple basic messages spoken very slowly. During this period a great many people were attempting to persuade him to stay on as an MP and this meant many meetings. 'Every encounter was a strain on me and I felt strangely diminished meeting people I had known before I was deaf.' During this period he was helped by his wife who refused to allow him to be shut out of things. They found a range of attitudes displayed from those who carried on a perfectly normal conversation, speaking directly to Ashley, while others attempted to use Mrs Ashley as an 'interpreter'.

> Since losing my hearing I had relied on Paula [Mrs Ashley] to help with people who could neither comprehend nor deal with deafness. Speaking clearly for me she eased the pressure of eye-strain and ensured that I understood the conversation. She firmly refused to allow people to ignore me while they talked to her – a natural tendency for those who could not be bothered to speak clearly. Whoever they were, working men or Cabinet Ministers, if they tended to push me out of the conversation in those early days they would be told politely but firmly 'Talk to Jack'. (ibid.: 145)

I can think of few social situations more calculated to give one a sense of 'diminishment' than to be by-passed in a conversation, and have that conversation relayed via an interpreter. For Ashley the insistence by his wife that people 'talk to Jack' paid off handsomely since he quickly acquired proficiency in lip-reading, although as he notes there are some speakers who are difficult to 'read'.

One of the contributions of the physically disabled is to sensitize us to the prepotent value-systems in society. Among these are the positively evaluated traits of health, physical power, sexual attractiveness and achievements. As role players we are esteemed according to our capacity as contributors to the economic role, the family role, the sex role. Disabled people collectively, though they are not a social group, appear to comprise the antithesis of approved values and effective social roles. According to Louis Battye the disabled haunt a 'unique sub-world with its unique set of referents' (1966: 8). Among the factors that make that world unique is that relationships are tinged and altered by the disability. For example, he notes that the nature of friendships between 'normals' and 'disabled' are qualitatively different from 'normal'-'normal' friendships (while acknowledging that profound friendships can exist). In relationships the constant struggle is against diminishment. The disabled appear as half-made, incomplete parodies of 'real people', and this incompleteness extends from the physical to the psychological domain. The relationship task for the crippled person is always how to be taken seriously as a man. Here is Reginald Ford (muscular dystrophy) discussing one kind of relationship.

A cripple learns eventually to be very wary in his relationships with women. Many women . . . think they are perfectly safe mothering or sistering anyone suffering from an apparently incapacitating disablement. They are genuinely embarrassed and shocked when they find their protégé has normal masculine feelings . . . They feel set down if he reacts in a normal way and many a beautiful friendship has ended in protestations of injured innocence and misunderstanding on one side, and on the other deeper bitterness and disillusionment. Pity is no basis for any but the most temporary and superficial relationship. (Hunt, 1966: 41)

This is one area where considerable improvement seems to have taken place; or at least it has become a factor in considering the needs of disabled people, but there is still considerable prejudice (Greengross, 1976).
As Hunt notes:

In his encounters with society the invalid rarely meets active dislike or disgust. But if he ventures into the world of love such feelings are not far off. It happens, on occasions, that a disabled person falls in love with a normal member of society. Sometimes it happens that that love is reciprocated. It is interesting to observe the different reactions to such − one is tempted to say − a social outrage. One gets the impression that the invalid has committed a more or less indecent act . . . The reaction is not apparent when invalids marry each other. The invalid may marry another of his kind. (ibid.: 50)

Intimate relationships between two disabled people, or 'mixed' relationships where the disability of one partner is known and incorporated into the relationship from the outset are now, though, more frequent and more socially legitimated than ever before. A relationship where one of the able-bodied partners becomes disabled, though, has been seen by Musgrove (1977: 101) as being placed under considerable stress, with the likelihood of divorce and separation being strong. His small sample of severely handicapped people did show a high incidence of relationships which had been damaged by the presence of disability but whether this would have been true for a larger and more representative sample remains to be shown. However, it is clear that more tolerant attitudes to sex, together with the belated emerging understanding of the sexual and emotional needs of disabled people, have helped to create a climate in which such issues are being discussed and some forms of help are being made available. In 1973, SPOD, the committee on sexual and personal relationships of the disabled, was formed. It refers people to counsellors in their own localities. Since then there have been several major conferences and a growing literature for both disabled people and their professional helpers. A list of useful addresses can be found in Hale (1979: 274) together with a concise bibliography. One of the recommended sources is the excellent *Entitled to Love*, by Wendy Greengross (1976), in which will be found a detailed and sensitive exploration of issues mentioned here only in brief. There is a growing literature on 'sex and the handicapped' and a gradual infiltration of the concept that people with a disability require a sexual relationship as well as many other kinds of relationship. Studies have shown that following spinal injuries sexual feelings are only slightly diminished in male patients and if anything increased in female patients. Recent studies (Dalton, 1978) have shown that physically disabled girls menstruate earlier than normal girls, though other studies have shown the physically handicapped as possessing much less knowledge about sex than their able-bodied peers. Only in recent times has counselling on sexual matters been seen as part of the total therapy needs of the patient, although there is still a primary tendency to perceive disabled people as neutered.

In terms of everyday social behaviour disabled people complain about being treated as incomplete. This expresses itself in the attitudes of others who behave as though the disabled person does not have a personal opinion worth expressing, and can be talked over and about as though invisible, deaf or without feelings.

> Like this . . . one is being pushed in a wheelchair and meets an acquaintance who with effusive greetings bends down to one's eye level to shake hands. He, or more probably she, then stands upright and addresses the chair pusher who is of course standing at the same height. Imperceptibly the chair is edged forward until the two are together behind it and are in a position to engage in an interminable conversation from which one is totally excluded. And matters are not made easier when one's attendant begins to move the chair slightly backwards and forwards in the unconscious rhythm of a mother with a pram. (ibid.: 41)

Ford (in Hunt) describes unexpected encounters with disabled people as a 'test of manners'. The other person stares to make sure that his eyes are not deceiving him, and catches himself doing it; or, recognizing a disabled person at a distance, deliberately avoids glancing at him for he may believe that the disabled person is also feeling that he is too distressing a sight to be looked at, setting up a 'vicious circle of hyper-sensitivity', but this can be broken into by 'trained self-confidence'.

It has been observed that one of the social tasks imposed on handicapped people is to be ready with an account of themselves. I saw and heard a lady strike up a conversation with a young man who had been carried into her compartment (for once someone had made sure he was not dumped in the guard's van). She quietly but forcefully put the young man through a catechism of his condition, causes, prognosis, all most well intentioned no doubt. Fortunately it didn't last long. As she got off the train something of the undeclared annoyance of her fellow passengers may have been felt for she exited on the line: 'It does them good to have a chat about things.' It had certainly done her good.

It is my impression that the current generation of disabled young people are more secure and confident in handling social situations and are not shy of making their feelings and values known. Like the group of children in wheelchairs in a school travel party who one morning went round and round the deck of the liner chanting in unison and very loudly, 'Yes, we *are* enjoying ourselves. Yes, we *are* having a good time.'

Summary

Disability is public property and one of the concerns of disabled people is their everyday treatment in society. People who are unable to mask or conceal their impairment appear to communicate some additional message about themselves. Social behaviour between the able-bodied and the disabled can produce a measure of unease, especially if the former have little experience of the latter. Many of our impressions of others in initial encounters are based on the most obvious and superficial data, and with people who are disabled the most obvious datum they communicate is their disability. A part of the difficulties in interpersonal behaviour may be the lack of a secure repertoire where customary automatic skills of eye-to-eye contact, proxemics and degree of affect are perceived as inappropriate. Such awkwardness may only relate to initial encounters and it should be stressed that people who are disabled are often adept at helping others through this awkwardness barrier. Just as importantly disabled people are no longer willing to be passive recipients of whatever interactional process the able-bodied are prepared to employ, being increasingly active in rejecting stereotypic expectations.

5
Caregiving and caretaking

The most obvious form of caregiving is that from parent to child, although whether mother-child bonding is instinctive and biological or a learned response is a matter of conjecture. Such caregiving involves in the early years the almost constant attention of at least one parent. This role requires little or no explanation: it exists unquestioned and the structure and purposes of the role are equally clear: to guard, nurture and encourage the unfolding of the child's potential to be both unique and at the same time a member of his society. The absence or weakening of this care structure appears to have several negative implications (Bowlby, 1960). More recent studies suggest that a minimal amount is necessary to form the attachment bond and beyond that what is crucial is the *quality* of the parent-child relationship (Bossard and Boll, 1966).

A second 'ideal type' of caregiving is that of nurses to their patients. Here we enter a different type of relationship, one in which the care given is a crucial element in the task and which is in effect institutionalized. It is not seen as intuitive, instinctive and 'natural' but 'comes with the job'. Unlike the mother-child relationship, the nurse-patient relationship has a degree of ritualism, of professional limits, and the quality of the relationship is reasonably well understood and its boundaries known to both parties. If the mother-child relationship is unlimited and functionally diffuse and broad in its affective colouring, the nurse-patient relationship is more functionally specific and emotionally constrained. The difference between these two types of caring roles is that the one is personal and the other professional.

The giving of care, aid and comfort is part of what is rather inelegantly called pro-social behaviour. There are many theories concerning the origin and function of pro-social behaviour. For example, there are altruistic responses which are situational and

71

others which appear to be evoked by particular stimuli. Some forms of pro-social behaviour are occasioned by transient feelings of well-being, while on the other hand there are individuals who seem to have a well-developed 'altruistic sentiment' that cuts across situations, specific stimuli or mood. It has been claimed that pro-social acts can be the product of feelings of personal inadequacies and inferiority finding temporary relief through a charitable act which bathes the insecure ego in a warm glow of momentary superiority. Also, pro-social behaviour may be the result of the impact of religious teaching or moral beliefs which place unselfishness and concern for others into a devotional or philosophic framework (Krebs, 1970).

Pro-social behaviour offers a challenge to psychological theories of human behaviour which have emphasized the significance of struggle, domination and self-enhancement as the prime motives of conduct. We know that our society is in part based on an ethic which gives emphasis to self-sufficiency and independence, status and success, power and wealth; and while it acknowledges that there are disadvantaged individuals and groups whose needs can legitimately be met, there is a survival of belief in self-sufficiency such as to make the recipient of public and private assistance feel subordinate and inferior. To require help is to be inferior, and to ask for it, base. More media coverage is given to 'social security scroungers' than to the significant under-claiming of welfare rights.

The individual act of concern, of giving to another, embodies moral, religious, social, psychological, legal and aesthetic ideas (Titmuss, 1970). However, the concepts of help become more complex when they are institutionalized. The individual act of pro-social behaviour may be placed alongside collective aid in which the personal and structurally unsupported act is embedded in concerted and collective behaviour of a purely voluntary kind, and alongside such behaviour we have the paid altruist. Such salaried altruists are persons who discharge a social obligation for the rest of us. By salaried altruists we mean those persons who have taken on as a job, tasks which society regards in an ambivalent way, often managing to combine lofty regard with menial returns. This ambivalent attitude is reflected in the discrepancy between publicly expressed esteem and low prestige. A headmaster of a school for disabled children once referred to 'clean' and 'dirty' work and said that in his school the dirtiest work (both unpleasant and arduous) was the least rewarded financially and socially. For someone to take on 'dirty' work is to become a part of the ambivalent notions we have about the value of such work and the value placed on those who do it. It is part of this confusion of values to question the motives of those who take on such tasks and to invent moral categories – unworldly, saintly, over-compensating, finding gratification in being superior – to explain a willingness to find a role in association with the stigmatized. ('I *do* admire you for doing it. I know *I* simply could not.') For just as there are those who would wish to place themselves well outside the contamination zone, there are those who actually seek to enter it.

Goffman in his *Asylums* (1961) writes about the mental patient entering a hospital as going through a changed moral career in which he experiences radical shifts in the beliefs he holds about himself, through initiation rites, dispossession of property, and various forms of mortification and regimentation. These changes are wrought by the institution acting through those who do the 'people-work'. Just as the mental patient undergoes a change in moral career, so there is an analogous change for those who enter people-work. The bank clerk who becomes a social worker, or the graduate in physics who becomes a careworker in a hostel for the disabled are both likely to be targets for speculation as to their motives: do-goodery is almost always problematic and questionable. Once embarked on their work they will be subjected to the counter-equivalent processing of professional indoctrination, rites of passage and the learning of appropriate language-value codes in which to express themselves to patients (clients), fellow professionals and the general public. Whereas for many occupations the rationale for the work is apparently self-evident (financial, status, enhancement of personal development, etc.), people-workers have to 'explain' their choice of occupation and this leads to a variety of defensive and apologetic responses. 'You have to be dedicated to do your kind of work' leads to a foot-shuffling, modesty forbids disclaimer. Compassion for hire takes many shapes such as presenting a tough professional aura concealing a heart of gold, or a tough professional aura over a heart of flint, the 'just another job' attitude, the routinizer and the emotionally insecure with their avid identification with the

stigmatized whose weakness and inadequacy are daily nourish-
ment, and where meeting others' needs meets one's own. Caregiving can be a vocation, a job or satisfaction of psychological needs.

Caretaking

There are occasions when the receiving of care is legitimated.
Infants, the sick and the elderly have their care as of right. Beyond
these occasions society requires the adult to take care of himself,
and in essence this is the meaning of adulthood. Those who
require long-term care through incapacities of various kinds are
under no illusion as to what being in care costs them. To be fed,
dressed, taken to the lavatory, wheeled about, lifted or carried is
to have a major portion of one's adult status diminished. The long-
term effects of prolonged caretaking are probably varied and
unpredictable, but it may be speculated that a limited behavioural
repertoire involves more than the loss of physical skills associated
with self-help, for these are symbols of status and identity.

> The disabled person . . . usually receives more help than his
> normal counterpart. His physical needs may have to be
> administered to and the responsibilities he ordinarily shoul-
> dered, may have to be taken on by others. The disabled is thus
> on the receiving end of helping acts, and he must adjust,
> accommodate and respond to being an object of aid; he is thus a
> helped person. (Thomas, 1970: 257)

The valid stance for a disabled person is to be one who is helped
but not to become a 'helped person' – a status which places
dependency over personality. Being trapped in the position of
requiring considerable help may have the effect of changing
perceptions of the individual so that he or she is viewed as an
object with care needs which through repetition and conditioning
change the individual's view of him- or herself and the 'helped
person' status is internalized and accepted.

Caregiving and caretaking are a convenient shorthand for a
complex reciprocal role which presents a number of personal and
ethical issues. For example, if we think of a young person with
cerebral palsy living in a residential community, he or she may
need help in many areas of daily living. In putting up an effective
struggle to sustain an image of adult-like independence the person
may 'manage' the help they receive by a measure of distancing.

We see the same mechanism used by hospital patients who are used as 'cases' for medical students on consultants' rounds, where the patients may distance themselves by 'withdrawing' from their bodies, mentally detaching *themselves* from their body which is being examined or prodded.) By distancing, the person receiving help seems to designate that help as being given to his body but not his self: a daily chore that is best regarded as routine. For caregivers that 'routine' may be central to their perceptions of their role but perhaps the most difficult aspect of care is the issue of gratitude. Should the caretaker be thankful for the care they receive? Should the caregiver expect gratitude?

It has been noted by students of institutional life that there is an ever-present danger of the dependency of the caretaker being used to develop a value system in which childlike needs are re-cast so that he or she is seen as childish – in effect, infantilization. As Jones (1975) noted in her study of subnormality hospitals, there was a tendency among some nurses to treat their patients as 'their' children; with the rights of reward and punishment which parents customarily feel they have over their own children, together with an expectation that the child-patient will be grateful to the 'nurse-parent'. It is exceedingly difficult to find principles which should guide the behaviour of professionals who are obliged by the nature of their people-work to manage the boundaries between their professional role and personal involvement.

It is one of the themes of the sociology of institutional life that inmates, patients and prisoners are shaped by the institution in ways which permit the staff to exploit their work role and functions in ways which are personally and professionally satisfying. This shaping may be most powerful in those insti-tutions which have minimal contact with the mainstream of everyday life and where prestigious, collectively powerful authority is set over a relatively docile, dependent and socially fragmented clientèle. This shaping may be unplanned in the sense that it simply arises out of the behaviour of staff who find ways of performing their roles which are efficient and economical, or may be a deliberate act of policy and therapy, as in institutions practising behaviour modification or using a token economy. But in both cases the way the institution is run is primarily for the convenience of the staff.

Frazer, telling the story of St Dunstan's, recalls the pioneering

efforts of Arthur Pearson to help the blinded victims of the first
world war. Pearson believed that visually handicapped
servicemen's pensions would spare them the worst effects of
poverty but that they would drift into 'useless lives'. He was
convinced though that this could be prevented by training and
the learning of a useful skill. The success of the venture was
considerable. Pearson believed that hostels with training facilities
would be places where men could learn to be blind! (Frazer,
1961). (*The Sunday Times*, August 1980, also carried a story about
the threatened closure of a mobility centre for the visually
handicapped entitled 'Learning to be blind'.) Robert Scott (1969
has argued persuasively that blindness is a learned social role, and
that this learning is acquired in three ways: a) in childhood and
later we acquire and incorporate certain views about blindness,
blind people and other stigmatized groups and this knowledge is
'available' to the person who loses his sight; b) the blind learn part
of their social role in face-to-face encounters with the sighted; and
c) they learn how to behave as a blind person within the
organizations established to help blind people.

The latter he describes as a complex latticework of agencies and
resources which are crucial for blind people as locations where
specialized help, recreation and vocational skills can be learned.
The specialized personnel staffing these resources he calls
'blindness workers' who not only have the key to these resources
and skills but also have a core of belief about blindness, blind
people and their rehabilitation and these core beliefs guide
behaviour.

The approaches are expressed as the blindness workers'
expectation of the attitudes and behaviours of those they are
trying to help. For blindness workers one key indicator of the
success of a rehabilitative endeavour is the degree to which the
client has come to understand himself and his problem from the
worker's perspective. While he learns to understand himself
from this perspective the blind person is also acquiring
blindness-related attitudes and behaviour patterns that 'go
along with' his rehabilitation. Thus it is that through the same
mechanisms that operate in personal relationships, many of the
attitudes and behaviour patterns and feelings at the core of a
blind person's self-concept are learned in the context of
agencies for the blind. (Scott, 1969: 19)

Minton's book has many parallels with Scott's view. In it he describes his experiences of learning to become a 'blind person'. On first meeting a rehabilitation worker he was told 'You can't hope to earn anything like the money you used to earn', and was then offered 'twenty employment pigeon holes for the blind' (from basket-weaving to computer programming) and comes close to believing that this represents the finite possibility of employment. At this initial interview he was given the tranquillizer of bureaucracy. 'You'll have to trust them – they have the experience.' He was given background information on the courses he could take, and he asked 'Does every blind man go through the same process of learning as every other?' By this time he was becoming wary of the experts' view which was crystallized in the phrase '*inmates* arrange their own concerts' and was also told that they elected a 'captain' to speak for them. Apparently his misgivings were justified, as his account of the 'purdah of blind care' of being processed and treated according to a standard pattern shows. He is not only critical but also deeply appreciative of some of the training (especially typing) he received, although he has some harsh things to say about his mobility training, which assumed he had no sight, whereas he had some residual light discrimination. Minton's active refusal to comply with the given blind role led to accusations of ingratitude and he was told: 'This place isn't run for your benefit.' Any institution having invested in particular training methods is reluctant to modify them. Hannah Wright (1978) describes the RNIB Braille method of reading as 'dated, insensitive, and extremely boring in content, paternalistic and narrow in concept and too cheaply produced to be efficient'. In spite of some evidence that only a few newly blind become efficient Braille readers and 'the rest of us become blind illiterates' the system continues to be offered, although it is being reviewed. The point to be made here is not to enter the argument about Braille but to see it as just one example of the way in which caring institutions can programme their activities albeit benevolent in intention to serve the needs of the institution rather than the needs of their clients.

Obviously rehabilitation involves the learning of new skills and these skills have to be taught by someone who is probably a better teacher for having faith in the methods and content being taught. But there is an important distinction to be made between the situation in which the learning of new skills that are acquired and those where the new skills become a major determinant of an externally redefined self. It is possible to learn Braille, use a long cane or a wheelchair as valuable but essentially pragmatic solutions to problems of mobility or communication. When this happens they extend the person's life-space, but when the skills are taught and conveyed as a facet of institutional ideology within the confines of a location already functioning to fulfil selective prophecies about clients, the skills are not simply functional prosthetics, they become identity markers, a visible signal of learning to be handicapped.

We get a clear idea of this process of care systems transforming themselves to suit the needs of staff rather than clients in the way helping organizations define their work and the priorities they establish within their area. One way to do this is to examine the age, sex, social class and regional distribution of a handicap and then to examine the way the helping organization allocates its resources. Scott did this for the blind in America and concluded that resources allocated by blindness workers were primarily directed towards child and the employable young adult who were mainly blind with no other handicap. But the distribution of the blind population showed an overwhelming preponderance of middle-aged, elderly and the blind with additional handicaps: as he put it, 90 per cent of the agencies were concerned with 30 per cent of the blind population. The blindness workers define their care role as centred on education and employment and the 'remnants' are seen as marginal. For Scott the agencies were rigid and resistant to change: their investment in traditional skills – 'Braille and mobility' – meant that large sections of the blind community were untouched. For Scott, blindness workers showed a greater commitment to their agencies than to blind people, while the agencies themselves were engaged in a displacement of organizational goals 'substituting for the legitimate goal some other goal for which it was not created and for which funds were not allocated', and among its changed directions was a preoccupation with bureaucratic procedures. Care agencies always believe in developing the client's abilities to the full, but since what is possible is controlled by the ideology of the system, what he does achieve is what he was capable of achieving.

Care – community or cloister?

A measure of uncertainty exists over the ideology of segregated residential facilities for disabled people. For some segregation is anathema, to others desirable, and for many a pragmatic, if not a perfect solution to a difficult problem. A residential institution is one 'providing a more or less permanent, and more or less adequate substitute home for a group of inmates who are cared for by a group of staff' (King, Reynes and Tizard, 1971: 37). Enclosed communities exercise a measure of fascination for the outsider as the well-marked boundaries provide an intensified theatricality and where the roles and rhetoric, the under-life, the play of power and personalities provide a riveting spectacle. As complex organizations, institutions offer examples of distinctions between manifest and latent functions, the moral careers of inmates and the roles of staff members.

The traditional territory of sociologists of institutional life – prisons, 'mental institutions' and subnormality hospitals – has led to such institutions and their styles of care being regarded with scepticism and outrage and to the development of expressions of positive affirmation of the value of community care. Perhaps, as Hunt has written, residential facilities for disabled people are part of society's inability to face sickness. They are places where social obligations can be discharged with the minimum inconvenience to the rest of us. For Miller and Gwynne (1976) residential institutions for the chronically sick and disabled appear to possess two contrasting value positions which they label humanitarian and liberal and are expressed in two contrasting institutional styles: horticultural and warehousing. In the 'humanitarian' régime the institutional ethos stresses the basic task of the maintenance of life for as long as possible even if 'life' has to be defined in a very narrow technical sense. In such institutions the interactional style for staff is 'keeping cheerful' and for patients, gratitude and stoicism. In the institution dominated by 'liberal' values, belief in the importance of attaining 'normality' is the goal no matter how desperate the circumstance of the person; normality can be achieved by changes in society's attitudes and the prevailing ethos is one of hope. However, Miller and Gwynne suggest that in such institutions the protestations of the normality of the handicapped person is contradicted by staff behaviour, for 'any inmate who takes too literally the liberal protestation that he really is normal and who behaves accordingly by trying to cross back to the other side, quickly discovers his mistakes' (p. 83). The liberal and humanitarian ethos is associated with two styles of care: horticultural and warehousing. The horticultural mode stresses that progress can be made by the patient and the primary task is to develop capacities and to cater for unsatisfied needs. Staff strive to encourage greater independence in patients. The warehousing mode accepts the inmate as one of life's casualties whose condition is life-long and moulds the inmate into a 'sick' role.

How far we are still wedded to the old Victorian asylum principle may be seen in the statistics for the mentally handicapped, where today some 55,000 patients (including 5000 children) are in subnormality hospitals and only about 7000 in community-based hostels and other strategies of a more familial dimension. Of the 55,000, it has been estimated that it is only of the order of 5000 who require custodial care for their own and others' protection. The large institution has many problems; it is often badly designed and located in out-of-the-way sites making visiting and social training difficult. It is often said that large institutions actually inhibit staff from carrying out their task as trainers of social skills, since the sheer numbers of patients and organizational routines pressurize staff to meet the needs of the institutional timetable. It is easier to dress a patient than wait for him to button up his shirt. If bathing takes place between 7–8 pm, and you have ten difficult patients, it is quicker to bath them than to let them do it for themselves. It is said that not only are new skills not acquired, but habits laboriously acquired quickly fade away through lack of practice. It is easy to understand how dependent, inarticulate and unsupported inmates can be shaped by the priorities of the more powerful professional staff. Miller and Gwynne describe many longstay patients in residential homes for the disabled as largely unquestioning about their environment or the decision made for them, 'inhabiting a shrunken world'.

Elizabeth Marais (1978) has described one aspect of the problem of residential care with her account of Peter, a young man with a history of being labelled educationally subnormal and a background of being unfavourably compared with a clever older sister leading to frequent moves from school to school.

Eventually a family crisis led to Peter running, or rather riding, away from home on a stolen bike – not an uncommon crime in the university town where he lived.

'However it is one thing to "borrow" without permission if your IQ is 120 +, but a very different matter if the label ESN is attached to you.' After a series of minor offences he was placed in a subnormality hospital under section 10 of the 1959 Mental Health Act. His IQ had been variously estimated as between 75 and 105. It was the stigmatizing label of ESN coupled with parental rejection which pushed Peter into an institution.

> The damning label ESN, so arbitrarily attached to him in early childhood proved impossible to remove. Since his parents displayed no willingness to have him home and obviously felt their problems were finally resolved by hospital admission . . . he continues to live in a locked security ward in the hospital with adult men many of whom have committed serious crimes . . . It is not the fault of anyone employed at the hospital that Peter has been committed to their care but no one is making any very positive efforts to find a better solution . . . We are always faced with the argument that there are no alternatives for misfits . . . [but] the longer he stays in an institution, the less are his chances of rehabilitation. (Marais, 1978: 267)

Peter is just one example of how people who gravitate into the world of enclosed institutions are lucky if they can discover someone to speak for them and are relatively powerless as individuals to counteract what is happening to them.

The experience of being helpless in the face of the power of care agencies is one which Terence Wells (1978) has written about. His career extended from a school for the educationally sub-normal, to a school for the partially sighted, a Centre for the Disabled, a social rehabilitation centre and an RNIB rehabilitation centre (where his report described him as 'bad-mannered, inarticulate, unintelligent and generally unemployable'). But he was able to write the following:

> I would play outside in the playground with other children. I often fell over but my mother thought it was playful excitement. When I went to the local primary school at four years old the teacher found I could not do many ordinary

things such as doing up shoe laces, finding my way around the school, or see drawings on the wall or letters on the blackboard. I also had great difficulty in learning to read – more so than the average child.[He was recommended to go to a school for the ESN.]

It was there they discovered that I had poor vision. (Wells, 1978: 21)

On his experience in the Centre for the Disabled he writes:

When I got there I found the other people were deaf, dumb, blind and epileptic. Most of them had more than one or two disabilities. They were all over sixty. The work they gave me to do was raffia mat making and pulling rubber handles on bicycle handlebars. (ibid.: 21)

He concludes his account, 'I especially want to go to college, I enjoy studying economies and politics'.

Wells' career contrasts with that of Peter's: the latter was locked into an institution while the former was moved from agency to agency.

One of the most perceptive accounts of the experience of care may be found in Frank Musgrove's *Margins of the Mind* (1977). In it he describes the life and experiences of various groups of adults who have undergone a significant change of direction and identity. One of these groups were patients in a Cheshire Home and they and the Home provided an opportunity to reflect upon 'the consequences for personal identity of the omnipresence of death', on Goffman's views on the resocializing of inmates, and whether the inmates would receive and accept the 'institution's definition of themselves and their situation . . . of waiting in the ante-room of death, while time itself might change its meaning in such a context'.

Musgrove saw the Cheshire Home as a refuge, a protected enclave on the margins of the world, but it was a refuge sought with relief and a sense of privilege by the 'residents'. Given the marginality of the Home, sociological theory might predict it would become the base for a counter-reality whose institutionally constructed identities were manufactured quite at variance with the identities of the residents prior to their illness and admission. What was found was 'a quietly tenacious normality'. It was a quieter more muted form of normality but nevertheless recognizable. Musgrove states that in general three categories are used to give shape and meaning to our lives: sex, age and occupation. These were used by residents though their time perspectives made the past very shallow and the present infinite.

The majority of the sample interviewed (fifteen) had had a period of normal, healthy life before becoming disabled (multiple sclerosis, spinal chord disease, industrial accident, stroke and cerebral palsy) and among their occupations were schoolteacher, shop manager, factory worker, nurse, motor mechanic, marine engineer, cook and lorry driver. They had been in the Home from thirteen years to a matter of weeks. Many had spent considerable periods in their own homes as a disabled person. In the interviews residents proclaimed the survival of their normal selves and this is helped by the management style of the Home. Residents felt that as they had been selected for a place this was a distinction, and the way they were treated enabled them to be grateful but not dominated. The staff were seen as skilful, unfussy and giving personalized assistance, and residents were not processed through the day in groups.

> This isn't a hospital, this is our home. The only thing wrong is you don't have your own front door key. You can go out when you like for as long as you like . . . You can have visitors all day long. You know that if you tumble you'll be missed and they'll come looking for you.

What the Home provides is a strong sense of a guaranteed future in which care, companionship and security will be provided. A minority reported they were bitter and unhappy but this was in contrast to the majority. The majority did not show that 'moral fatigue' which Goffman thought characterized institutional socialization, instead they demonstrated the survival of the 'biographical self', a continuity of identity.

> I like it here, there's just enough people. You don't just become a name or a number. You retain your individuality. You can stay as you are, which you can't if you become one of dozens or hundreds.

The survival of the biographical self and the fight against a handicapped identity results in relationships within the Home being kept shallow. Friends and relatives from the outside are the ones with whom residents can talk about intimate matters and when a death occurs 'the pattern of life and relationships is not deeply disturbed'.

In spite of the duration of their illness residents are anchored in their former roles; work is seen as a potent image of identity and the rupture of their working lives was the factor that made them marginal, not their disability *per se*.

> If it wasn't for not being able to get about [middle-aged man, paralyzed] I'm as normal as anyone. I haven't changed my outlook in the ten years I've been paralyzed. Life is much the same in or out of a chair. The only thing is, you can't do what you want to do when you want to.

In spite of being in a wheelchair or bedridden, sex and age were crucial factors in residents' biographies and the impression given is of a view of the self halted at the time of the fracture of their normal roles.

> The far-distant experiences before the onset of illness were the ones on which they focused their minds, and which were frozen in the gaze of their attention. In their marginal world occupational identities stood firm in the presence of death, and age-sex categories retained their significance in a world which was officially neuter. But temporal perspectives lost their linearity and a circular present sat precariously on a deep past which contained everything of real importance. . . . A future leading out of an eternal present did not exist. Personal futures were the most taboo subject in the Home. (Musgrove, 1977: 103)

Given the potential for moulding vulnerable and dependent people to routines which make life easier for staff, this seems to be one (and it cannot be an isolated example) institution where the staff and residents seem to have evolved a philosophy of care in which the individuality of the resident survives remarkably intact and should be contrasted with the mass processing of inmates in our large chilly depositories for the unwanted.

One of the prime tasks for administrators of care facilities for the handicapped is to unburden themselves of the shackles of traditional concepts of care which have evolved from the asylum and the hospital. The work conducted by the Wessex Regional Health Authority (Miller, 1977) in setting up hostels for the mentally handicapped is a good example of how a new vision can radically change existing perspectives. This was provided by Dr Kushlick and his research staff who began the process of unpicking traditional warehousing models of care through carefully planned observational studies, by refusing to consider generalizations such as 'this patient is a nursing problem', and asking what is the *specific* difficulty? and by attacking comforting professional anodynes such as 'allow the development of potential of handicapped people in all settings and particularly in hospital and other settings'. His approach was to focus on a specific behaviour, supply interesting activities and place patients in a home-like environment with parent-substitutes not nurses: a blindingly obvious set of answers that required real genius to supply. The differences this quality of care makes to the lives of mentally handicapped people is perhaps impossible to quantify, but subjective impressions lead to beliefs that the change is desirable and has a positive outcome.

The sociology of institutional life portrays a grim picture of degradation ceremonies, soulless routines, loss of independence and the gradual weakening of the self-image until it conforms to institutional expectations. While there is truth in this perspective there is also the view that human nature is more resilient than we sometimes imagine. Cohen and Taylor (1972) found that long-term prisoners in a high-security gaol did not lose their identities as a result of being processed by the prison system. The support for their identities was sustained by the prospect of eventual release and while a similar tenacious hold on identity was seen in the Cheshire Home, the grip there was on the past.

This survival of identity is most vividly seen in the history of Joseph Deacon. A spastic with a severe speech impediment he spent his formative years and most of his adult life in care establishments. Only in recent years did he develop a way of communicating with one close friend and with the aid of another friend, Mr Deacon, presented his autobiography *Tongue Tied* (1974). The very existence of his book is a small miracle but from it we may take one point, namely, that prolonged exposure to care régimes does not appear to have processed Mr Deacon out of a strong sense of self. One of the intriguing aspects of his book is the powerful sense of a continuity of identity. The small boy in Camberwell surrounded by his family survived as a member of that family – he may be a displaced family member, but is not an institutionalized zombie. His account is full of family reminiscences as well as anecdotes about his hospital friends, such as a glorious day out to attend a wedding.

> When I got there I was surprised to think how many people knew me – Peter's brother, sister, uncle, aunts, on Peter's side. My friend Ernie [his 'translator'] was good to me when he understood me in front of these people. I don't know what I would do without him. We had drinks and we had a disc-jockey. We stayed for two hours. You see what a time I had. At seven o'clock we toasted the bride and Linda fed me champagne. (Deacon, 1974: 41)

A life apart, yes, but not apart from life.

Nancy Kerr (1977), a psychologist who is also disabled, suggests that care establishments respond to particular questions that disabled people 'ask'. When a disabled person is admitted he or she begins to ask certain questions of themselves and of the institution. There will be questions about *identity*: Who am I? Am I the same person as I was before admission? *Practical questions*: Is it tough to get about in a wheelchair? *Vocational questions*: Shall I be able to work? *Role questions*: Can I do anything to help or shall I put myself in your hands? And *status* questions: because I need so much help, does that make me inferior or childish? Kerr suggests these questions are often unspoken but answers are found in the style of care offered by the institution. Some institutions answer these questions in the following way: 'You are a second-class citizen; getting about in a wheelchair is no problem at all; no, you can't get a job but we all pretend you can so just go along with the charade and keep up the rug-making; just leave it to us, we know, we're the experts and yes of course you are dependent and the more you are the happier we both shall be.' Other institutions respond to the unasked questions with something like 'You *are* the same person; it is tough to get around but we'll show you how to cope and we need a lot of help from you; getting a job is very hard, it can be done but if it can't we'll tell you; we can't do anything unless you are with us and if you feel inferior, put down, tell us, because we've made you feel that way. You're an adult in a wheelchair.'

Kerr, from her own experience, knows what happens to handicapped people:

> I have been wheeling along to treatment settings in various parts of the country, attending to my business as a teacher, researcher or clinical psychologist when an attendant or nurse would bustle alongside and challengingly or sarcastically say, 'Hey, where do you think you're going?'

Sometimes this could lead to a free lunch.

> On more than one occasion my wheelchair has been hijacked by an attendant who, without comment, wheeled me into the dining room of his institution. (Kerr, 1977: 47–54)

Those we like to help

Experimental evidence suggests that the giving and receiving of help is a complicated social event. This was neatly illustrated in an investigation by Katz (1978). He obtained four groups of people to participate in trying out a new test. In this task they were led by a 'normal' person who was pleasant, helpful and considerate, by a 'normal' person irritable, cold and abrasive, by a 'disabled' person who was 'nice', and a disabled person who was 'not nice'. After completing the tasks the participants were invited by the director of the project to help the person who had been conducting the trials to complete their assignment. Offers of help were given in the following order of willingness to help (most help–least help). The most help was offered to the unpleasant disabled confederate, then the 'nice normal', then the nasty normal and last of all to the 'nice disabled' confederate. Can you suggest an explanation for this finding? Also you might like to mull over the implications for disabled people. Caregiving and caretaking have been looked at primarily in the context of residential and institutional settings where the personal and professional issues are at their sharpest. Almost nothing has been said about these matters within the family and home, nor of helpers and the helped in public places. Beyond these there is the whole question of the physical environment which might be described as planned obstruction, designed to maximize the need for help. More optimistically much of the current literature on practical aid for disabled people is increasingly stressing aid as a function of increased independence, and among a wealth of resources we can select the *Aids for the Disabled* (DHSS), *Coping with Disablement* (Consumers' Association) and Lowman and Klinger's *Aids to Independent Living* (McGraw-Hill). However, it is not always possible for people with disabilities to cope with daily living problems even if aids are readily available. With age some are unable to sustain even a modest degree of self-management and for the able-bodied old age and decline of capacities are inevitable.

Disability and ageing

Much of the professional literature on disabilities concentrates upon childhood, adolescence and early adulthood, while charity appeals, the media and other forms of impression-making are similarly inclined to neglect the substantial numbers of middle-aged and elderly people who face equivalent or greater difficulties than their younger counterparts. The comparatively new science of gerontology has redressed the picture of the elderly as a neglected group, distant from social life and who in extreme old age are destined for institutional life. As Laslett (1977) observed, the experience of old age depends on a range of factors such as the job one has retired from, the skills of the individual, one's health and economic position. The very real sufferings of a minority, and especially of those who come into contact with social services, do not represent the conditions of the elderly in general terms. However, surveys like those of Isaacs, Livingstone and Neville (1972) do show the massive increase in hospital and community health resources required to provide a service for the most severely disadvantaged, sick and disabled elderly, and case studies, like those of Robb (1967), and recent newspaper stories testify to the sometimes callous treatment that can be the lot of the powerless in the hands of caring people who are over-stretched or simply unimaginative, whether in the state or private sector. Another part of the picture is the stress which can fall on families and hospital and nursing-home staff in looking after dependent, disabled, incontinent and sometimes very confused relatives or patients.

Impairments and disabilities in the elderly appear to carry a different social and psychological meaning from similar handicaps in the young – handicaps in old age are seen as part of the general handicap of old age. Yet there is no reason to believe, and indeed the very opposite may apply, that physical deterioration, loss of mobility and independence are any less important or psychologically less painful in someone of advanced years than in the young. According to Vischer (1978) the experience of ageing is a compound of physical and psycho-social factors in which the physical factors are generally seen as more significant than the social and psychological ones. Reactions to ageing range from denial and depressed resignation to a gradual realization that capacities for new experiences are dulled, coupled with and increasing fondness for recollection as a cognitive mode.

While acknowledging the importance of the elderly as a group it is not possible here to do more than give a single example. Fortunately it is both an acutely observed and well-written account. In her compassionate, yet cool and ironic book, Ellen Newton has provided us with an authentic and faithful insider's view of the process of being elderly and infirm and of giving up one's home, and all that that implies. In *This bed my centre* (1980), Ellen Newton describes how, after an active life as a broadcaster and writer, in her seventies she was forced by angina to enter a series of nursing homes. In these she kept a confidential diary in which she recorded her life in bed, her thoughts and feelings about being old, the way the old are treated and those aspects of her life from which she was shut off by her condition. 'Bed', she writes, 'as a residence is not a thing to cultivate.' In spite of being in a nursing home set in beautiful surroundings she missed everyday sounds ('young people speeding recklessly home from late parties . . . children calling to each other as they race down the street') and was irritated by being treated as an object. She mourned the loss of her own place and possessions and felt the hurt which came from the loss of independence. Here she writes of going to the shower: 'a sister escorts you from your bed in a very clever chair with a seat exactly like a life-belt. Sitting in this minus night attire of course, you are wheeled into the shower recess and speedily soaped, rinsed and dried (Newton, 1980: 20). The phrase 'a very clever chair' is just perfect.

Through her observations and reflections she comes to the

view that many of the so-called characteristics of elderly people, and especially of those in institutions (even the most benign), are formed by routines and attitudes which encourage just those forms of behaviour which should perhaps be discouraged. For her the degradation of 'ceasing to be a person' was one which she was able to resist with her wit, intelligence and her diary, and while she was able to discharge herself at eighty-one to begin work on a novel, for most of her fellow patients there was no such reprieve.

Many of the themes which Ellen Newton develops are almost identical to those found in accounts of disabled young people and those who have not been able to secure a place within the community. The similarities between the experiences of old age and/or disability are those of exclusion from the mainstream of life, a constriction of roles, limitations of opportunities and a progressive decline in self-directedness which gives way to a manner of life increasingly shaped by others. The assumption that the elderly feel any the less intensely the loss of former capacities needs to be resisted as strongly as the imputation of 'abnormality' to the young disabled. Lack of space prevents a more detailed consideration of the many issues surrounding the elderly handicapped person. But it does seem as though publicity and professional interests tend, inadvertently, to make us think too narrowly of disabilities as prominently the province of the young. Nothing could be further from the truth. The range of diseases, impairments and disorders which afflict the elderly (arthritis, Parkinson's disease, strokes, sensory losses, mobility problems, incontinence, memory loss and confusion et al.) are each worthy of detailed consideration in relation to how they affect the sufferer, the family and community services. One issue which links the range of conditions in those elderly who become handicapped is the manner in which they are treated by others. It is the experience of many elderly people to be treated as though age implied a deterioration in capacity to make rational decisions and more and more parts of their lives are colonized by others. The patronizing and condescending attitudes which are sometimes displayed towards the elderly are reminiscent of the experiences of younger physically disabled persons.

Summary

The person who is disabled is likely to require help over and above that which we all need. The situation for a person needing additional help in a society marked by the value it places on independence can create problems of status, moral worth and identity. Where legitimate care needs are handled with a lack of sensitivity there is the possibility of that person being placed in the category of a 'helped person', that is, as one whose independence and freedom of choice are further constrained. Where caregiving is institutionalized and does not arise out of friendship or family ties the caregiver is also potentially vulnerable and both may find their behaviour conditioned by the institutional definition of each other's roles. An example was given of a residential setting for disabled people in which the caregiving and caretaking were orchestrated in a way which devalued neither party. The manner in which residential establishments manage the care of residents conveys powerful information about their values – whether they are developmental or custodial, encouraging individuality or suppressing it, designed for residents or for the staff. Here again significant changes may depend upon the abilities of disabled people to influence the quality of care they feel is right for them in a new negotiated order.

6
A new life

The birth of a handicapped child or the subsequent discovery of a defect or an irregularity in development produce ripples which extend from the parents, to the immediate family, to relations and friends, to medical, educational and social services and to society as a whole. The impact of abnormalities is wide-ranging for birth is not only a biological event, it is a social occasion for which an intact, undamaged, physically perfect child is part of a web of expectations involving not only the parents, but also professionals who have monitored the mother's pregnancy and delivery. The perfect child is a vindication of parental and professional roles.

The most neutral term we can use for this event is stress – stress for the doctor who has to tell parents, stress for the parents themselves, and a stress which at each such birth raises thorny medical, legal, ethical and social issues. Sometimes this stress is immediate as when a child with spina bifida requires a life-saving operation, perhaps within the first twenty-four hours of life, and parents have to come to a major decision when both, and especially the mother, may not be in a condition to make a rational decision. The issues are more easily raised than answered. Is survival the only criterion? How much do we value 'quality of life'? Does society pressurize parents into a lifetime of care for their handicapped child? Are such decisions best left to the family, or do professionals have a role? For example, should the doctor guide parental decisions? Who is his patient – the child or the child's family? How do you feel about withholding medication or surgery from a baby and calling it a 'management option'? Differences in attitudes and practices are illustrated by the life-chances of infants with spina bifida where presenting similar diagnostic features: those born in the Midlands had a 90 per cent chance of death, whereas those in Baltimore had a 75 per cent chance of survival.

Hauerwas expressed one of these issues thus:

> Many parents seem to assume that they should be responsible
> to bring children into the world in a manner that can ensure
> their happiness. Parents tend to think that not only should
> they be responsible for meeting their children's basic needs,
> but also must see that they do not have to suffer. Parental
> responsibility extends to assuring their children a happy and
> successful life. Convictions like these reduce the options at
> birth to a perfect child or a dead one. (Hauerwas, 1975: 28)

These are options which amniocentesis and ultra-sound examinations make possible.

There have been many studies of parental reactions to the birth
of a handicapped child and in one of these (Ellis, 1974) twenty
couples with a spina bifida baby (open myelomeningocele) were
seen by the medical team in the twenty-four hours after birth.
Only three of thirty-four personally seen by Ellis had any
knowledge of spina bifida. During the interim parents were told
of their child's handicap and the child's future was discussed
including background information on the effect of the lesion on
mobility, the urinary tract, skeletal abnormalities and hydrocephalus. An initial prognosis was made and the possibilities of
future pregnancies mentioned as well as the care problem that the
child would present and difficulties in adolescence. Following
their discussion parents were left to digest and discuss what they
had been told and were encouraged to talk things over with a
close friend. For some parents the medical advice indicated that
surgery was not thought to be a wise choice. Eight couples
requested surgery even though contra-indicated. Of these eight
babies, two died within two months, one is in a wheelchair
attending special school, two are in normal schools and three, not
yet of school age, are making reasonable progress. Twelve couples
did not request surgery and eleven of these babies died. One
child's case was reviewed after two months and treatment was
started. Contrary to much received wisdom, Ellis found many
parents capable of rational decisions even in times of great stress,
calling upon hidden reserves of willpower that enabled them to
think clearly and act wisely, although parents may need time to
re-think initial responses as this example shows:

> The wife of a physically fit, well-housed couple in their middle twenties with a healthy daughter aged two-and-a-half, gave birth at home to a daughter with spina bifida. [Following a consultation at the hospital the father signed the consent form. The operation was delayed until the consultant was able to see both parents.] During a talk with the doctor . . . he said, 'Doctor I can't go on with it,' and when asked why it was he had changed his mind when only a few hours earlier he had requested the hospital to do everything possible . . . he replied with great frankness, that he was very much in love with his wife and was devoted, as she was, to their little girl. But there was, he continued, a history of mental illness in the wife's family and twice in their short married life, he was aware that his wife had come near to breakdown. (Ellis, 1974: 72)

He realized that the strain of a handicapped child would be too great for the whole family and that the new baby would not get the care and attention it might need. In the course of a further conversation the wife made a comment similar to her husband's. After a private discussion the paediatrician was called back and informed that they did not want the operation. The baby survived for about six weeks.

No one could envy the responsibility placed on the shoulders of doctors who have to counsel parents at such a time, and it would be a brave person who could pronounce on the right way to break such serious news. There have been studies (e.g. Tizard and Grad, 1961; Moss and Silver, 1972) which have attempted to find out about this critical time and how parents were told. It is difficult to evaluate retrospective accounts since the shock of disclosure may make memory unreliable or subsequent difficulties with the child may be perceived as due to initial lack of tact, sympathy or understanding. But the impression gained of this episode is that many parents look back on it as a time in which the blow was delivered in a clumsy, cold or clinical manner, although as Mary Sheridan (1973) notes this may be a way in which the doctor manages his own emotional vulnerability.

The baby is alive

With gross malformations medical personnel often have immediate knowledge of the baby's handicap. The cumulative excitement and joy over the prospect of a child has to be terminated. I know of no account which in a few stark sentences communicates better this experience than that of David Mason (1976). Mason is now well-known for his energetic campaigns to secure a reasonable level of financial recompense for thalidomide children.

Mrs Mason's pregnancy was uncomplicated and being a fit woman in her early twenties, there was no reason to expect anything else. Her only minor difficulty was a restlessness which made sleeping a problem and she was given some tablets to help so that she could wake up feeling refreshed and able to face the day. For seven months the pregnancy proceeded normally except that at a routine examination a medical student said he couldn't detect any limbs on the foetus, but a consultant put him right. Meanwhile Mr and Mrs Mason went through the ordinary preparation of a couple expecting their first child — buying a pram, a carry cot and decorating the nursery. Since the baby had not arrived on the expected date Mrs Mason was admitted to hospital and underwent a long labour. Labour had begun in the morning and by midnight Mr Mason was anxious and visited hospital with friends carrying the ritual bunch of flowers.

> Twenty minutes passed. Then a young doctor emerged with the sister. I saw her nod towards me and the doctor, after glancing briefly in my direction, took off his white coat and hung it up. Then he walked towards Paul and me, looking at the floor as if unwilling to catch my eye. My heart sank. Was something wrong? Was the baby all right? Was Vicki all right? . . . We sat down and the doctor opened up by saying, 'There have been one or two problems.'
>
> I broke in. 'How's my wife?'
>
> 'Your wife is perfectly all right.' He seemed to be relieved to say it.
>
> 'And — the baby?' I asked.
>
> 'The baby is alive,' he said.
>
> (Mason, 1976: 18)

The doctor went on to tell him that the baby was not completely developed, not ready to be born: her arms and legs were not complete 'and one or two other things as well'.

Mr Mason describes his first meeting with his daughter.

I saw a tiny torso with what appeared to be flowers sprouting from the corners. The little face was marked from the middle of the forehead and across the nose, lips and chin with a bright wine stain; the nose was so flat as to appear deformed. 'Surely,' I demanded, 'you're not going to allow a child like this to live?' (ibid.: 18)

The doctor was calm and said, 'Mr Mason, I can't help you.' Mrs Mason now knew that something was wrong but had not seen her daughter or been told, and was given a sedative. Mr Mason left the hospital.

'Suddenly I felt a deep personal shame that my child had been born with such deformities. I considered it could be blamed on the physical make-up of myself and Vicki, and I had an insane impulse to keep secret what I thought of as our imperfections', and he tells his friend that the baby had died. Going on to see his family doctor he learns that *Distaval*, the sedative, had been linked with the birth of children with malformations. Mrs Mason was pregnant in the autumn of 1961. *Distaval* had been withdrawn from the British market in November 1961.

'What do you think is wrong with your child?'

For parents with an obviously physically handicapped child, the confrontation is immediate, but there are other disabilities which are not so easily detected or detectable. Some impairments only become apparent when regular developmental milestones are not reached. However, there is a condition which we might call 'planned parental ignorance', where doctors, nurses and health visitors are fully aware that the child presents an atypical picture yet are reluctant to communicate their views to the parents preferring to allow the idea of handicap to emerge and be stated first by the parents. This has the advantage that the first active step in re-labelling the child from normal to handicapped comes from the parents and not from the medical bureaucracy. It allows a slow build-up of realization that all is not well while at the same time permitting the development of a firm bond of attachment between mother and child enabling acceptance to be more probable. Here is one example of such a tactic.

Mrs W. was eighteen when her second child Sally was born. Mrs W.:

> She was born at home, with the cord round her neck and was a deep purple colour: she had oxygen at home. Right from the start I knew there was something wrong, she had really ugly features, she wouldn't feed properly. She always snuffled and had sticky eyes. When she was three weeks old, we thought she should be properly examined . . . My mother had asked the midwife if Sally was mentally handicapped and the midwife said 'It's more than we dare say, we can't commit ourselves'. . . . at the hospital they asked me why I wanted her examined and I said I thought there was something wrong. They asked me what, and I said obviously I didn't know or I wouldn't be asking them; I just wanted her to be thoroughly examined. They did this and asked me to come back in a fortnight. I saw a specialist who said 'What do you think is wrong with your child?' I said I had no idea, and she said I must have or I wouldn't have brought her here. I said I had no idea at all. The specialist said I must have some idea, and I said, 'No I don't'. I got quite annoyed, she was just pressing me to say what I thought, and all I could say was that I thought there was something wrong, with all the vomiting and the eyes. Eventually I said my mother thinks she's mentally handicapped and the specialist said 'Your mother's right, she's a mongol' [Down's syndrome]. She said she'll never be independent or marry, never hold down a job, and will always be a responsibility to me. Maybe I'd think about having her put in a home – but this was never further from my mind. (Fox, 1974: 22)

Asked how she would have preferred to be told, Mrs W. said

> I'd have liked to have been told in the first few days, because in those eight weeks so many horrors went through my mind that weren't necessary. Nobody had mentioned the possibilities of mongolism until that woman came out with it. Some people may be able to hide things from themselves for years, but I couldn't and I needed to know. (ibid.: 22)

It can happen that the delay in appreciating that the child is handicapped is not planned at all. Mary Green (1966) with one child at primary school was contented with her new daughter and living a quiet isolated existence with few other babies around for comparison and she thought Elizabeth was just a placid infant who was no bother. A seaside holiday produced an event which altered that view as a small baby walked away from its mother and Mrs Green found out that this active child was 9 months old, while 10-months-old Elizabeth was contentedly asleep on her pillow. Although the baby who walked was doing so at an age well before most babies this did not prevent Mrs Green from noting the contrast between this very active child and her daughter. Gradually she began to look at other children and to make comparisons, and only then did she and her husband admit to each other their private concern. Eventually when Elizabeth was sixteen months old the family obtained a medical diagnosis of Down's Syndrome. 'In those first moments the doctor's verdict was a relief. The taboo word was said, our fears voiced and confirmed' (Green, 1966: 15). Elizabeth was momentarily changed into a new role, an abstraction called Down's Syndrome, but that perception was quickly changed by the reality of a 'grubby bundle calling for its breakfast'. Following the medical verdict Mrs Green recalled a surge of energy in which she wanted to get everything sorted out and wanting to tell everyone. On the surface she had accepted Elizabeth's handicap but

> I began to realize that underneath I was feeling very different. Something very black and bitter was making itself felt. Elizabeth was a mongol. Our daughter made with so much love . . . was a freak, a not-quite, a runt, useless and pointless. Any other animal would let its weakling die or deliberately destroy it. That is taboo for human animals. We had to care for and cherish her like a normal child . . . We were morally bound to rear this runt, this peculiarity, who would always be a burden to someone. (ibid.: 19)

Such feelings are found in the experience of many parents coming to terms with their new problem, but Gail Stigen (*Heartaches and Handicaps: an irreverent survival manual for parents*) expresses it better.

> Discovering the concrete fact that you have a handicapped child is a heart stopping, mind boggling, gut level body blow

Some parents get it socked to them right at birth. Others get it later. Some accept it, some reject it, some buckle under the strain, some rise above the fact. (Stigen, 1976: 6)

But as Ann Lovell in *In a Summer Garment* (1978), a sensitively written account of bringing up an autistic boy, recalls, there is an indeterminate phase where there is tension between the suppression of knowledge that something is seriously amiss and the simultaneous desire to have the unthinkable given its right name. With rare conditions like autism (four in every 10,000), and with the variety in child developmental patterns it is not surprising that expert opinion is cautious rather than impulsive. She suggests that it was quasi-official policy to withhold diagnosis until the mother was in no doubt that she had a handicapped child. These tensions can make communication between the parents and the professional difficult to handle and it becomes tragically easy to mishandle the situation even with good intentions. In this excerpt we can feel the tension between the desire to know and fear of that knowing.

The interview with her will remain vivid in my memory. My hackles rose almost with her first question. Everything she said seemed to imply that I had mismanaged my children. No doubt she meant to imply nothing of the sort, but now I was growing sensitive on the subject of my strange son. She said nothing more direct in the interview than he seemed to be playing around the perimeter of the room in rather a strange way and I, furious now, retorted that it was probably because he did not like the room very much. And that was that. I sat there loathing her . . . I regard that piece of non-communication as tragic. If only the doctor had explained her fears — and the reasons for her fears — tremendous pressures would have been lifted from Simon, myself and my marriage . . . I would have started then and there to look for the help we sorely needed. (Lovell, 1978: 11)

If you only dip into the professional literature on parental reactions you will find written large the words 'Guilt'. It does not matter over-much that researchers have been seduced by this psychologically attractive form of 'victim-blaming', what does matter is that this view has become professional gospel for many social workers, teachers and care professionals. The usefulness of the 'guilt' concept is its universality. If parents appear to be unconcerned, it's because they're guilty; if they are concerned and push professionals too hard, they are over-compensating for feeling guilty and – the best Catch 22 of all – they can be described as attempting to develop a normal life-style as a mark for guilt feelings. My own theory about the 'guilt theory' is that researchers are uneasy themselves when confronted by parents. Please do not misunderstand. I'm not saying such feelings do not exist, but it is so easy to use a simplistic idea like 'guilt' as a convenient pre-packaged way of seeing parents. One way of developing a counter-view is to find out how parents of handicapped children react to descriptions of themselves provided by professionals. Here is Gail Stigen again after reading a manual on *Parents of Handicapped Children – their feelings and reactions*:

> I don't know which parents this esoteric manual had found to interview, but they didn't appear to be even remotely similar to anyone I knew. A bunch of whimpering, guilt-ridden, uninformed, misinformed, snowed, intimidated, documented mice. These apologetic, forelock tugging supplicants at the altar of professionalism were certainly not the parents I have come to know. (Stigen, 1976: 26)

It would be better to avoid stock, simplistic explanations of parental reactions for they are likely to be as varied and personal as any response to stress.

The significance of 'telling', using the 'taboo word' or having it 'socked' to one is to be found in the way in which this new definition of the child and his family (for now not only do we have a handicapped child we have a handicapped family) marks him and the family as occupying a changed status. The child has entered a new social category. Being officially designated a 'handicapped child' implies that people will respond to that child in strategically different ways from those if the label is unplaced or never placed; and as we have seen, the label is one that can be sought and dreaded.

While much has been written of parents' reactions, the overwhelming bulk of reports are focused on the mother. This is understandable for she has been through the period of pregnancy and birth, and has been involved in the care of the infant, and she is also likely to be the person who sees specialists, social workers and health visitors, and incidentally she is likely to be the one at home when the research worker comes calling with the question-naires. There is concern over how parents are informed and how they respond to this first information and from this concern there is evidence of the need for support and help. Many believe that the most effective prop for parents is another parent with a similarly handicapped child.

Perhaps there has been too much attention paid to initial reactions and responses. Perhaps what is even more important is the course of developing attitudes and relationships between parents and child, rather than first feelings. An amazing number of factors have been studied to determine which ones influence whether a parent will accept her handicapped child – the mother's personality, social class factors, race, religion, ethnicity, the age of the child, the nature of the handicap, the parent's degree of self-acceptance, the presence of other normal children in the family, the length and stability of the marital relationship and the expectation of the role of children in marriage. As you might expect all these factors have been found to play some part at some time for some parents. However, it might be thought that the extent and quality of interactions between parents and child would be one of the most fruitful sources of insight into parent-child attitudes and responses.

While it is relatively easy to appreciate at least superficially the work-load, care and anxiety that a sick or handicapped child imposes on a family, and it is relatively easy to comprehend how such daily and unremitting attention brings stress which can be handled by certain states epitomized by terms like rejection, perfectionism and over-protection, the propensity of pro-fessionals to find problems in such families rises to its apogee with the family who present as 'normal'. One of the things pro-fessionals find utterly disquieting is the notion of normality co-existing with handicap.

Birenbaum (1970) wrote that mothers of retarded children attempted to establish an apparently normal round of life which also involved treating the defective child as normal, but, said Birenbaum, normality with such a child is not possible, so parents substitute love and affection for a more instrumental goal – note the word 'substitute'. Voysey (1975) argues that the reason why parents of disabled children opt for this normal framework is that they have been socialized to accept it. She found that parents of disabled children *claimed* the child had not had a serious effect upon family life and were able to state this because parents were supported by religion, medicine, psychiatry and sociology, and through these sources learn that they are guiltless, acquire more maturity through having to cope with a handicapped child and became missionaries to overcome society's ignorance about handicap. These rationalizations include acceptance of the inevitable, abandoning the future (living day by day), the positive value of suffering, the worth of individual differences and true values ('There's more to life than just being successful'). This ideology of normality is sustained by impression management where collaborative efforts between family and child produce a performance which emphasizes normality. Underlying this and similar stances is the conviction that disability in children means a handicapped family and where obvious pathology of attitudes and relationships can be found the presence of attitudes and values associated with normality must themselves be a social mask.

The absence of pathology in parents has been shown in several studies (Goodstein, 1960; Boles, 1950; Hewett, 1970), although comparatively little emphasis to these studies has been given. For Voysey the acceptance of normality by parents was acquired largely through interactions with doctors and with the disabled child. It was through significant figures like doctors, that concepts of normality were mediated. Darling (1979) appears to argue that such support from technical experts will be incorporated provided it is in accord with definitions of the child held within the family or by important lay groups in the family's community. Booth (1978) writes that the family's perception of their child is largely formed within family and is relatively uninfluenced by external views. The impression which the professional literature seems obsessively to give is that of the family as a hopelessly damaged social system. From the delivery of the taboo word to institutionalization of the child, the family shares in the stigma of the child. Until we rescue the family from the benign intentions of professional categorization and stereotyping they will be perpetually cast into this state of vulnerability.

One of the ways in which attitudes to parents have changed in the last twenty years may be described as the gospel of the home. Whereas at one time it was regarded as not unexceptional for parents to reject their deformed child and to cast him out, the discovery of maternal bonding and the effect of separation and deprivation on young children have indoctrinated a generation of social workers and others as well as students with the view that the best place for the child is with his family and the role of society's agents is to keep the family intact and going. Adult mental well-being is premised on secure psychological foundation which can only be found by deep attachment to a limited number of adults with whom the child has regular contact. The excessive concern with the child's needs are sometimes seen as over-riding those of the mother or the family as a whole.

Thankfully, most parents are able to accept their disabled child, but it has been suggested that society exercises a kind of moral blackmail over parents so that negative, hostile feelings or wishes to reject the child and have him placed away from home are seen as signs of emotional immaturity and warped values. Fraiberg (1977) saw how the bonding between mother and child could occur, as it were, in a moment, and mothers expressed their feelings of love for the baby commencing with the first glance at the baby's face – a moment which was described as a sense of the baby becoming a person. Work with mothers of thalidomide babies has shown that decisions to institutionalize the baby could be reversed as mothers found 'the baby's eyes "looking back"', the "eyes talking" were moments recalled as compelling. The decision to keep the child was remembered . . . within the context of this engagement of the eyes' (Fraiberg, 1977: 96). But such moments of bonding can be contrasted with feelings of the darkest kind. Hannah Mussett in *The Untrodden Ways* (1975) recalls her feelings after the birth of a Down's Syndrome baby. Mrs Mussett had grown up with a handicapped sister and had taught handicapped children. The impact of the child on her other daughter and on the family as a whole was such that she and her husband discussed placing Lucy in a residential home. In the excerpt we find her discussing this possibility with a doctor.

He gave me his opinion, in the same quiet insistent voice he always used, that he was sure that all handicapped children should live at home with their families. He said he did not believe in separating such children from the community. H was sure that this was best for Lucy – she would get on just a well at home as away, and after all weren't all children th responsibility of their parents? Did I know how much it cost t keep a child in an institution? He assured me that though Luc was severely retarded, as she grew older she would fit into th family quite well – being only a little different from any othe child. (Mussett, 1975: 60)

On a second visit to the doctor Mrs Mussett brought the subjec up again and this time she wanted her child's case to be brough before the county medical officer.

He had, he said, to act in accordance with his own conscience and he would not recommend that any handicapped chil should leave home – unless it needed hospital treatment. 'Afte all,' he said, 'you are not the only one. I have child patient who are spastic or crippled or deaf, they are just as bad as your you know.' (Mussett, 1975: 63)

As far as the doctor was concerned Lucy was the responsibility o her family.

Mrs Mussett writes in her notebook:

You, society at large, have condemned my daughter to life. I would have killed her then, when they told me she was a mongol. Urged by the vehement instinct of a mother to protec her from a harsh, unfriendly world where she would be a stranger always and everywhere. Prompted by love, by pity by compassion, I would have killed her then. It is you, remote society, who uphold unquestioningly your rigid law – Thou shalt not kill, even for mercy. If she had been my responsibility – mine only – she would have been sleeping at peace now in the quiet village churchyard, with the winter-jasmine coming into bloom upon her grave as the last rosebud shrivelled with frost Oh that she had been exclusively my responsibility! – You – society at large – have condemned my daughter to life, and in doing so have made her your responsibility not mine: what are you going to do about her now? (ibid.: 60–4)

McCormack (1978), Hewett (1970), Gregory (1976), Kew (1975) and McMichael (1971) record the changes which a handicapped child makes to a family's life patterns. One way of regarding these changes is to see how conventional patterns are interrupted. For example, Farber (1959) has suggested that family life can be seen as a series of progressive shifts involving different emphases and roles, status and responsibility. This 'cycle' may include a) a childless couple, b) with children of pre-school age, c) with children of school age, d) with children who have left home, e) a couple on their own. Each stage is associated with roles giving a particular emphasis, and there is also a normal timescale associated with each stage. With children who are severely handicapped the family progess is arrested − or rather it may proceed at different rates with respect to normal and handicapped children. The detailed and demanding care-needs of a disabled child may be such as to anchor the family at an infant care level for a lengthy stretch of time. This temporal aspect is also reflected in the avoidance of the future as when families coping with many and varied stresses 'take each day as it comes'.

A new life for the family

The birth of a disabled child is not the only new life, for the family of such a child enters upon a new era. It is important to recognize that in writing in such a way there is a danger of over-emphasizing the distinctive nature of such family experiences. Indeed, I believe that a good deal of research has made it its target to unearth the distinctive as opposed to the conventional aspects of family life. So great is the concentration upon stress and practical and financial problems that ordinary relationships between parents and handicapped children appear as a rarity in the research literature − though they do exist!

We may readily understand why there has been this preoccupation since it is problem areas that demand attention from central and local government, voluntary agencies and parental self-help groups. Where consistently in survey after survey the same issues are raised, we can identify areas of need which demand attention. These can be listed as a) improved pre-natal care, b) more effective and widespread genetic counselling, c) skilled and sensitive informing of parents, d) immediate psychological support, e) immediate and continuous practical advice on all aspects of childcare, f) someone to act for the family in liaison with the multiplicity of care agencies, g) improved relationships with medical practitioners, h) better counselling over the school needs of the child, and i) parents as partners in educational programmes and opportunities for parents to meet with parents with similar experiences.

So many and varied are the problems facing parents and society that we sometimes lose sight of families that do make a good adjustment to their children; of marriages that are more firmly cemented as a result of shared concerns; of brothers and sisters who are not psychologically scarred by having a handicapped sibling; of parents who meet professionals who can relate to them without the asymmetry of power and status, and of decisions affecting the child where the parents are genuinely consulted and play an active part. The distorted image of parents and professionals with a picture, on the one hand, of psychological insecurity, unreasonable demands and over-involvement, and on the other of indifference and callous procedure-ridden bureaucrats is capable of misrepresenting the complexity of reality.

In this section we shall be concerned with aspects of family relationships leaving to a later chapter issues related to contacts with professionals and services that are available to family.

While it is dangerous to generalize about the effects of a handicapped child on the family, it is legitimate to inquire whether such a child alters or affects relationships in the family. Among the changes are: a new definition of motherhood; the role of the forgotten father; and effects on brothers and sisters.

Motherhood

The model which has been most frequently employed in exploring the changes which a handicapped child brings to his relationship with his mother has been that of marginality. It has been thought that in developing a relationship the mother no longer has the support of the full range of intuitive and learned maternal responses which she might have used in respect of a non-handicapped baby. Instead she is tugged by the child's abnormality and his normality, and may focus upon his handicap or upon those aspects of his physique or person which link him to the normal world. Since there are no ready-made solutions to the problem the mother fluctuates between extreme views. As

Roskies (1972) has shown, with mothers of thalidomide-damaged babies, one of the critical elements in forming maternal responses is not the physical status of the child, but how both child and handicap are perceived by the mother and those close to her. For Roskies the range and diversity of maternal reactions to birth defects and of the developing relationship is as rich and complex as in any sample of mothers and children, and there was no standard or uniform response. Mothering a disabled child has many of the features of normal mothering and yet it does contain certain distinctive elements. Among the latter Roskies discovered an absence of a temporal developmental framework in which to consider handicapped children. Shortly after the shock of the initial information mothers were unable to grasp a view of their maternality except on a day-to-day basis. This temporal uncertainty may continue for many years, with the question from the child 'What will I become?' being among the most confusing, and may lead to an ambivalent perception of the future in which optimism and realism mingle uneasily. 'In the absence of a unifying structure provided by the concept of a life span, the element of time became a disorganizing factor rather than an integrated one. There was no continuity but only unceasing, unpredictable change (Roskies, 1972: 279). The uncertainty of the future and an ever-present sense of discontinuity is a major element in the mothering of a disabled child. This is not just the unpredictability of children reaching normal developmental milestones, but an even greater uncertainty about the social status of disabled people in society. The very trajectory of the family is uncertain and a cause of perpetual negotiation and re-negotiation. In the moments of personal crises – finding the right school, an appropriate job or a place to live – is embedded a more general question of a temporal frame for persons with an uncertain social pedigree. Our services are also based on short-term needs with the child-family needs chopped into concise fragments which again reinforce the discontinuity of the familial trajectory.

For those whose task is to encourage 'acceptance' by the mother, it may be most effective to focus on those aspects of the child with which she can identify as similar to herself and similar to normal children, and to 'underplay' the disabling, stigmatizing aspects. As Roskies notes, it may be psychologically wiser to allow tacitly a measure of denial rather than officiously to strive for realistic acceptance. Encouraging mothers to see and treat their child in as normal a manner as possible may not provide the best conditions for the child's development nor will it solve problems, but it may be the crucial first step in helping the mother rid herself of the notion that she is a handicapped mother.

The forgotten father

Husbands and fathers are often the forgotten piece in the puzzle of relationships within a family with a handicapped child. They are presented as shadowy figures during the period of initial crisis while the mother and child occupy the centre of the stage. Woodburn (1972), in a study of spina bifida, noted that with this handicap it is fathers who are first given the information and describes their reactions as similar to those of mothers which are more frequently cited in the literature. She records that the majority of families (84 per cent) were intact families at the time of the study and that the mothers spoke of the positive contribution their husbands made to care and management which was a significant factor in helping the family to cope with the child. In 1976 Cummings looked at three groups of fathers: those with mentally handicapped children, those with chronically sick children, and those with emotionally disturbed children. He examined how they felt about their children, how they got on with them, their satisfactions with family relationships, their attitudes to bringing up children and their personal self-esteem. Fathers of mentally retarded children were seen as less buoyant, more preoccupied, more depressed and having a lower self-esteem than fathers of normal children. The effects of continuous care schedules was seen in an emphasized liking for orderliness and organization. Cummings states that we may have under-estimated the psychological stress on fathers and that this stress may have profound effects on their personalities and relation-ships. He suggests that fathers may have fewer opportunities than mothers for compensative activities with the handicapped child, and there are fewer community resources for fathers. Cummings also hints that the masculine role gives less opportunity for expressing grief and frustration.

    Susan Gregory (1976) in her study of families with a deaf child, draws attention to the similarities with mothers and fathers in her sample to fathers of children with cerebral palsy in their degree of involvement with the family and the child. She also makes the point that high levels of paternal involvement do not necessarily mean consensus between parents on how to bring up children, and she makes particular mention of disagreements over matters of discipline within the home.

McCormack (1978) quotes statistics which reveal that among families with a mentally handicapped child the divorce rate was ten times higher than the national average, and in her book she describes marriages that have been broken, those strengthened and those perilously surviving. Among the many valuable points she makes (together with many vivid examples) is that the stress is unevenly distributed between husband and wife. At worse the father can simply be an uninvolved spectator, or he is made to feel superfluous to the all efficient super-mother. The arrival of the child throws the relationship out of balance, and parents may have little time or energy for each other, and may have wildly differing views on how to deal with the handicapped child. As one father said:

> It was years before I began to see my son as a child with a problem instead of as – well – an oddity. I remember having a row with my wife when she accused me of not liking him. I said, 'How can anyone like or dislike that – there's nothing there!' I suppose that was an awful thing to say and she has never let me forget it, but it was what I thought. (McCormack, 1978: 132)

Some marriages survive because of a sense of commitment to the child and not to the spouse, for 'being a single parent is no doddle at any time, but bringing up a handicapped child alone . . . can be incredibly difficult . . . Money is tight, leisure is nil, isolation everywhere . . . No wonder many couples put superhuman efforts into keeping their homes together' (ibid.: 133).

But there are also those marriages which emerge stronger for shared experiences, where tasks are more evenly shared and where mutual support makes it possible for a relationship to thrive in adversity.

Brothers and sisters

There are two extreme views on how having a handicapped brother or sister affects other children in the family. One view suggests that sibs relate well to the handicapped child, have a normal relationship and actually emerge from the totality of the experience as more mature, more considerate, more understanding and more realistic. The contrary view suggests that a handicapped brother or sister means being squeezed out of the centre of family concern, leading to jealousy; it means being unhappy because other children make fun of your 'funny' looking kid sister; and for some sibs, the concentration of pressure escapes into emotional problems, lower school attainments and psychosomatic disorders. Children may be torn between affection for a disabled brother or sister which they can show in the family home, and yet be very vulnerable to public occasions involving the whole family. McCormack gives several instances of teenagers not bringing friends home, or taking care not to be seen with the handicapped sib, like the girl who asked her father not to bring her retarded sister to her school parents' evening. As McCormack comments these are moments when the unitary nature of the family is threatened and precious beliefs about 'being one family' seems like self-deluding rhetoric. Woodburn (writing on spina bifida) seems to hint (but no more) that when parents were talking about the handicapped child, the normal sibs' feelings about their brother or sister were avoided or where it did take place, it was the parents who handed over their own philosophy of handicap ('no one in this world is perfect', p. 233), but there were parents who avoided such discussion.

The care needs of the handicapped child may accelerate normal sibs' growth into independence. One mother with two children, one of whom, Paul, was deaf, said in answer to the question 'Does a deaf child in the family mean that the mother gives less attention to her other children?'

> I try not to make the difference, but Paul automatically gets more attention from me because he needs me more. You see Peter's always been independent – *at eight months old he didn't really need me* – he was very grown up for his age. (my italics) (Gregory, 1976: 181)

Darling (1979: 62) summarized a good deal of the literature in this area which shows that the effect of a handicapped brother or sister depends on the nature of the handicap and the degree of parental anxiety created by the handicap, and that effects are sex-related. It appears that girls are more prone to adverse reactions, and this may be due in part to their greater involvement in the care and management of the handicapped child. Ann Gath (1974) has shown that whether a sibling is adversely affected depends on a complexity of factors (social class, birth order, family size and the age of the normal child at the birth of the handicapped child), and while this is a population 'at risk' of emotional disturbance such disturbances are by no means inevitable.

Coping alone and the disabled parent

Two special groups of parents require to be mentioned; the single parent and disabled parents. All the pressures and problems which can at least be shared within a marriage are shouldered by one person when a marriage breaks up. McCormack (1978) is one of the few writers who have included a section on the single parent family (pp. 133–41), and her case studies do indicate that the presence of a handicapped child is a factor but not necessarily the crucial one in the break-up of a marriage. Her study also shows some of the practical and financial problems which a mother on her own faces (e.g. not able to take a full-time job because of having to collect a child from school).

The *Source Book for the Disabled* (Hale, 1979) suggests that with the growing involvement of disabled people in all aspects of life more are getting married and are considering bringing up a family, although statistics on the numbers of such families are not readily available. Hale argues that the decision by a disabled couple to have a baby may be influenced by the opinions of relatives and friends, but that they should make the decision on their own taking into account what they can realistically manage. The extra effort involved for a mother in a wheelchair has to be considered, although there are many examples of disabled mothers coping in an excellent way. Hale describes and illustrates many of the adaptations to nursery furniture and feeding devices and gives suggestions on bathing, dressing and generally taking care of the infant. One of the most interesting parts of this section in her book consists of an outline of the problem of discipline and co-operation, of encouraging independence and guarding against common dangers. Although there are many practical and emotional difficulties for disabled parents, Hale presents a generally encouraging picture of family life when parents are disabled.

To conclude this chapter and make a link with the next, a transcript of an interview with a mother of a handicapped boy is given. Hewitt (1981) interviewed a number of mothers allowing them to dictate what they wanted to say – in effect, the interviews used the mothers' agenda. In the transcript below, Sue has two children; her handicapped son was her first child; she was 26 years old when he was born.

Sue's agenda

Normal pregnancy, no family history [of handicap], induction, gruelling labour, rotten high blood pressure. When baby was born, I saw what looked like a flat burn on his back. I thought 'Oh, he's done that coming out'. We'd never heard of spina bifida, because we never had – sounds ridiculous. I remember the fantastic atmosphere just before the baby was born. My husband said, 'Here he is, I've got my little footballer.' Everyone was pleased, then the atmosphere changed, it was as if it was chilled. They said, 'We'll take him over there and clean him up.' I knew something was the matter. I said 'What's the matter with you all?' They took the baby away. They were peculiar. I thought I'd done something wrong. I didn't realize they couldn't tell me until a doctor was there.

'Where's my cup of tea?' I said. They brought me a cup of tea. They left me there for two hours and told me the doctor wanted to see me, but he was changing a baby's blood and would come to me soon.

I thought the worst, you should be told right away, it's awful to be kept in suspense. My husband rang up all the relatives to tell them the baby was okay. Then the doctor asked to see my husband. He told him all the things that spina bifida meant, brain damaged, incontinent, the lot, and then said, 'Do you want to tell your wife?'

The nurse came in to give me an injection. I was getting to feel hysterical. At that time the worst handicap I'd known was a mongol. I thought he was dead.

My husband came in, he looked yellow. 'What's the matter? Quick,' I said, 'is he a mongol or is he dead?' My husband said 'He's not, he's a spina bifida. I know it's terrible but they can

do things about it.' He then told me a catalogue of events, the
doctor had told him. A young doctor came in, I looked at his
face, there were tears in his eyes. The fact that he was so upset
meant so much to me. He said, 'Has your husband told you?
Don't believe all you read in the newspapers.' The nurse said,
'Do you want to see him?' I asked, 'Was he going to die?' They
brought him in, he was a lovely baby, lovely skin, lovely
fingernails, perfect. Ironical, I can remember thinking 'How
come his little fingernails are so perfect?' They explained about
consent to operate. I asked them again, 'Was he going to die?' I
was told, 'No.'

He had to go to the Children's Hospital and he was
christened; they wrapped him up and I gave him a cuddle.

My husband said, 'We couldn't part with that little fellow.'
Mother thinks, 'Once you know the worst, you know what
you've got to face and fight.' My parents and sister came and
then went to the Children's Hospital. When my baby was
taken away I started to cry. I couldn't feel my legs because of
the drug and remember thinking and feeling guilty, 'He'll never
feel his legs.' The nurses tried to stop me crying. They've got to
do that, they don't like other people's pains. You've got to
grieve – they won't let you. A houseman came in, I remember
snapping at him, 'You needn't be saying give me a sedative, I've
had one.' Another young doctor said, 'Look, I've seen your
baby and he moved the left leg, so don't you give up hope.' I've
always clung to that. The other fellow gave him a look across
the bed and I knew he shouldn't have said that to me. I saw him
a few days later and thanked him for it. He seemed quite
embarrassed.

At the hospital, they didn't think he'd move his legs, but he
did later. I remember feeling drained, thinking, 'It must be one
step away from being dead. It's like floating on a cloud, if you
breathe, you'll die.' The nurse at this stage said, 'Things will
not look so black in the morning. Things never are.'

Everyone was kind. I was worried about my mother being
worried about me. They put me in a private room – too much
trauma. I kept waking up in a fright, kept seeing Mum's face;
didn't want my parents worried.

Nobody mentioned my baby in case it upset me. I woke up –
a heavy weight – like a dream. I thought then I must write all

this down, there must be a reason for all this. I kept thinking about my baby.

The next day a good friend and her husband came to the hospital. I was saying to them, 'Don't worry, I will be all right.' They didn't know what to say. All my family were upset. My Dad, he's a quiet man, he just burst into tears at the side of my bed.

My husband was great, he had to be the strong one. He geared himself up. It's an unreal world in hospital.

I felt baby would die after the operation. He was okay, it took a while to dawn on me that he was going to live. We discussed it. We loved him. It had been suggested by a midwife that these babies can rule the house, it's far better if they are put in a home. I was horrified by this. Mother-in-law said, 'You can't keep it.'

One thing I do regret, I was given milk tablets. I could have breast-fed my baby, it would have been best for him.

Nobody told me anything. Those days seemed like an age. Thousands of things happened. I became a completely different person. I asked to see the baby. The hospital rang the Children's Hospital who told me baby was well. Mother-in-law went to see baby, came back and said, 'It seemed mental to me, one eye went one way, one another'. Her own sister who is a nurse told her this was rubbish. Mother said she broke down and cried and cried.

My husband decided to go to work. He had to face everybody. Really, he had more to cope with and he was fit and able to muster his thoughts. I couldn't walk for a fortnight because of stitches. You learn to cope with the pain. It cemented our marriage.

They put me in a room next to the prem baby unit. I can remember thinking, 'I can understand how people who have lost their babies have an urge to pinch one.' I am not religious but am now convinced there is something else, it's weird. Trying to justify rational thinking. I remember just before I had Sam thinking, 'You've everything you want, good home, husband, everything, now you're going to have a lovely baby – what are you going to do with your life?' I felt as if I wasn't doing enough. I thought later, 'That's it – there you are – there's your challenge.' I felt it all fell into place.

I asked the vicar who christened Sam what the name meant, he said, 'Asked of God'. That's it, I thought. I knew then all this was meant to happen.

I was crying and depressed, but in the corridor I met another girl who'd just had her baby, I told her about my child. She said, *'So what, I'm a spina bifida and look at me now!'* To me I couldn't believe it – fantastic – it was as if just when I needed to be shaken out of depression, someone was looking after me. I asked the doctors if I could go home. I couldn't stand the hospital. They don't know how to cope, what to say. They don't know how to deal with it – it's an embarrassment to them.

At the Children's Hospital the surgeon spoke to us. I cried. I must have made a display of myself. I remember them giving it to us straight from the shoulder. They tell you the worst. I remember saying, 'Do they walk?' The doctor said, 'I have to tell you most people give up the struggle on callipers.' I thought you either sink or swim. It brings out the fight in you.

If it's physically possible for him to walk, he will. It made me more mature, a better person in the end. I've sent Sam to a normal school.

The handicap – physical – doesn't come from the family, that's showing he's different. I've never thought of him as different. We've brought him up as an ordinary child, because he is. The point is anything that made me sad, caused trauma, has come from society.

All along, I've had to fight for him to go to normal school. He has had to be educationally assessed. Other children are not. The Education Department assess.

He had callipers to his chest, then to his waist, nine operations, they do these things for a better quality of life for your child and then you have to fight the system. Even doctors; the attitude of hopelessness comes across. They can't believe it when they see him walking. The doctors are too matter of fact when dealing with a child already handicapped. They write off a fractured femur as just another thing, yet make a fuss of a child with a sprained ankle. In their minds I feel our children are sub-standard material. It comes across. They have low expectations of my child, I'm looking forward to him walking. When they first sent him home in callipers, I was given no help.

I just walked him round in his callipers but didn't even know if I was doing the right thing. I needed help then. I rang up the Spina Bifida Association. They lent me parallel bars, a 'physio' came out. I used to put a chocolate drop on the end of the bars. I eventually got him walking with a frame, I walked him round for hours. Then I pestered for waist callipers. They told me he couldn't have them as the muscles didn't work. I argued they wouldn't if they were not used. Again I had to fight the low expectations of doctors. I took him to school, the Head refused him, he was labelled. I wrote to the Chief Education Officer. I told him if my child was black, Chinese, etc. he wouldn't be refused admittance to the school, so why my child? The Deputy Education Officer arranged with a Head to accept my child.

I remember when I was pregnant again and Sam was in a broomstick plaster, it was difficult – going back to the callipers, I had him walking within a month. Then I pushed for below-the-knee callipers. Now, he has just elbow crutches. The doctor did apologize and said, 'I'll take my hat off to you, he didn't appear to have the strength.'

He can crawl, he does little and often. It doesn't bother him. I go to school at lunchtime and change him. We think when he's older he'll learn to express himself. Going back to the hospital, we've waited two hours just to see a bone specialist, he comes along with his array of students, doesn't even speak to you, talks to the students, about our child not to us. My husband made the comment: 'You wouldn't get away with this in industry.' The doctor remarked, 'I think you ought to leave this up to us.' I think you need to be tough, dedicated, prepared to fight. Make yourself an aggressive person to get your rights and put your points of view over. Allowances mean little, but they do mess you about.

I think acceptance by society will get better. As far as possible he's integrated. When they grow up, the kids will accept my child as Sam, not a physically handicapped child. This is why I feel it's important they go to normal school. (Hewitt, 1981)

Summary

The birth of an impaired child is an event which can be regarded as significantly changing the lives of those closest to him or her. It is one of the most painful events that any family can experience as countless testimonies witness. Every such birth renews the issues of survival, quality of life and questions of priorities – which comes first, the child or the family? For many mothers the events surrounding the birth of a handicapped child are recalled in vivid detail. Other parents come to a slow realization that the child is not developing normally and in both cases adjustment is a highly personal affair, but fortunately the vast majority of parents work through this difficult time and emerge with accepting attitudes. Parents of handicapped children have been the subject of simplistic concepts like 'guilt' and 'over-protectiveness' and insufficient attention has been paid to the quality of relationship which develops between child and family. The constant care-needs of severely disabled children present a continual drain on parents' physical and emotional resources, while the special circumstances of the family will imply changes in conventional roles for mothers, fathers and siblings. The difficulties of intact families are often great but perhaps even more so for the one-parent family. In recent years the subject of the family where the parents are disabled has received some attention and there is an impression of a generally encouraging picture in this regard.

7
Parents and professionals

Parents of disabled and handicapped children have to deal with a set of needs arising from their child's developmental difficulties which are often of a kind and magnitude which cannot be met from the available resources within the family. These needs may be categorized as information, understanding, medical, social, psychological, educational, vocational, financial and practical. Families can be faced with comprehending the nature and cause of a handicap, understanding how the disability will influence the child's development and with involvement with doctors, surgeons, hospitals and many agencies. The family may find the handicapped child presents emotional problems to parents and brothers and sisters which require help from social workers, and if the child has a learning problem psychologists may be called to assess him, which in turn may lead to relationships with special school teachers. Finding the right vocational preparation or a suitable course of further or higher education, may link the family with yet another set of professionals, while the search for the available funding for families via the maze of social security and other sources of help presents yet another area of interaction with the agents of bureaucracies. The practical requirement of having a house adapted for a child in a wheelchair or getting some short-term relief for parents with a twenty-four hour a day responsibility can again bring parents into contact with a further group of professionals.

Identity and definition

One of the important outcomes of parental-professional relationships concerns the shaping of parents' concepts of the identity of their child, and their understanding of disability. There are two very different views about this shaping process. One perspective suggests that professional definitions of the child are remarkably powerful in giving parents a view of their child.

Darling (1979), in a review of research on parental attitudes to handicapped children, lists a number of factors which have been implicated in forming their attitudes. These included traits pre-existing in the parents prior to the birth (e.g. mother's personality, social class, race, ethnicity and religion), as well as influences subsequent to the birth. While many studies have shown that family reactions and family life are greatly changed by the presence of a handicapped child, there have been others which indicate that family life is very similar to that experienced within families without such a child. Clearly where families have been able to construct a normal routine, even though heavily involved in bringing up a handicapped child, they are of considerable interest. Interest in this aspect has focused on 'claims' to normality, or the rhetoric that the family is 'just like any other family' where, as Birenbaum (1971) has attempted to demonstrate, the claim to 'normality' appears to involve a shift of child-rearing strategies (e.g. in the case of mentally handicapped children, parents shift from the more instrumental aspects of socialization, to more affectively tinged interactions). Voysey (1975) in an examination of parents' views of essentially 'normal' family life asserted that parental views are markedly shaped by the terms, concepts and interactions with 'significant others'. She saw religion, medicine, psychiatry and social work as providing a measure of supportive legitimation of claims to normality. Further support comes from voluntary associations, stories of successful family patterns, and from parental organizations with an investment in de-pathologizing the parenting of handicapped children.

Timothy Booth (1978) argues a contradictory view. Instead of seeing, as Voysey does, parents having their view of their child shaped by professional encounters and professional definitions, he suggests parents deal with the diagnosis of handicap in highly individual ways but which are essentially ones in which parents are attempting a resolution between professionally given definitions and their everyday experience of living with a child who is not a clinical category but a person with strengths and weaknesses (as we saw in 'Sue's Agenda' in the previous chapter). In this process, suggests Booth, it is the manner in which parents handle this resolution that is more potent than the clinical definition provided by professional experts. Although this view is one which has considerable appeal in the way it asserts the emergence, survival and eventual domination of a naturalistic and humane view of a child, rather than that of medical specimen, it does seem likely that the amount of effort required to arrive at this perspective (a child who is handicapped) will be affected by the professional opinions offered to the family. The psychiatrist who said to a mother of an autistic boy, 'I see this as a disposal problem', or the paediatrician who informed a mother of a baby with spina bifida, 'Don't take him home he'll never amount to anything,' are both offering an identity for the handicapped child which will make the emergence of a natural perspective that much harder. Indeed so vulnerable are parents during the period of identification of handicap, so uncertain is their understanding of the child's problems and their own emotional reactions, that the preferred professional version may appear to be the one security in a time of uncertainty.

Help starts here

Although it has taken many years to develop, society does recognize that the family with a handicapped child is a social system which may need help. Below are some examples of the kinds of help which can be available:

1 Parents can refer their child to a District Assessment Centre.
2 Genetic Counselling Centre.
3 Health visitors, physiotherapists, occupational and speech therapists.
4 Social workers (local authority or hospital based).
5 Parents' groups.
6 Voluntary organizations.
7 Allowances claims, DHSS leaflet HBI (*Help for Handicapped People*).
8 Local authority power under the 1970 Chronically Sick and Disabled Persons Act, to pay for adaptation of domestic dwellings.
9 Attendance allowance (DHSS leaflet N1 205).
10 Free milk for a handicapped child of school age not attending school (FW.20).

11 Grants for extended education.
12 Supplementary benefits (low income families).
13 Family fund.
14 Orange badges for special parking facilities.
15 Mobility allowance.
16 Hospital fares (low income families).
(Source: Voluntary Council for Handicapped Children (*NCB* 1976))

While such a list gives an impression of a comprehensive service, of agencies and resources simply waiting to swing into action, what the booklet *Help Starts Here* makes clear is that parents have an active role to play in securing the right kind of help for their children. Parents are advised to 'consult a paediatrician early', are told 'physical and mental handicaps can often be lessened if action is taken early', 'not to be afraid of asking doctors and therapists to explain things more than once if they do not understand' and 'you play a key role in helping to improve', 'don't shut yourself off from friends and relatives . . . explain to them', and get the message that passivity is not the watchword. But what emerges quite clearly from this booklet is the idea that being a parent of a handicapped child has all the appearance of being a career. It is a career in which parents are likely to meet a wide range of professionals, and parents may have to learn certain social skills in relating to these professionals. Stigen (1976) goes so far as to suggest that parents will need to perform the expected role of 'handicapped parent' in order to secure the necessary services for their children and to put on an impression which will be congenial to the service providers.

An uneven balance of power

In most parent-professional encounters there is an uneven balance of power, a differential of emotional involvement and an unequal perception of reciprocal needs. While professional help is available and does make a constructive contribution to helping children and their families, the nature of professional-parental encounters presents the potential for conflict. This conflict is represented by a decidedly distorted relationship in which the balance is tilted in favour of the professional. Professionals are by definition experts in their own field; this gives them a legitimate authority in those areas which are marked by the boundaries of professional training, experience and competence. Against this legitimate authority the parent is seen as 'lay', ignorant and uninformed. One of the ever-present dangers in these situations is that the professional will see the child as possessing characteristics and symptoms which are within the professional's boundaries and on which he may pronounce as to causation, diagnosis and treatment, but while doing so he may fragment the child along the boundary lines of his own discipline. The parent may have difficulties in reconciling this fragmented view with a more naturalistic, holistic view of the child experienced through daily living. Another potential problem area is that the professional may be encouraged by his personality or institutional norms to use routine solutions, whereas each handicapped child and his family present challenges to organizational and conceptual flexibility. The expert sets up his technical authority against the global experience of the parent who is often uniquely qualified as the world's only 'expert' on his or her child. Most typically that expert knowledge is discounted.

The struggle to find the right kind of help is often an exhausting process for parents but once having made the right contact they will have an extremely high degree of emotional involvement in the encounter. For them the precious hour in the consulting room will be a major event; what the expert says, how he reacts to them, the tone and climate of the interview, and the non-verbal communication through posture, social distance, gestures and expressions will be attended to with care. On the other side, for the professional, this interview or consultation is less emotionally charged, more routine and part of his day. For the parents the consequences of the interview can be life-shaping and they will be fully aware that it is not just their child who is being regarded but their moral worth and technical competence as parents and people. For parents the interview is loaded with emotions, hopes and anxieties but equally crucial they will see the professional as having access to vital resources which may be denied if the relationship between them becomes strained.

Gliedman and Roth (1980) suggest that where parents reject professional views then professionals are able to use a number of defence mechanisms to explain parental opposition. One such method is through 'psychological' explanations (parents are not 'rational' because of their anxiety or guilt), a method Darling (1979) called 'victim-blaming'. For Gliedman and Roth the characteristics of the parent-professional relationship were that professionals behaved as though parents were ignorant, even irrational, and that their role was to be passive and receptive, acting as enforcers of the professionals' dictates. These who challenge this role can be denied services or are liable to be perceived as in need of help themselves – they too have become the professional's clients. Beyond this there is yet a further possibility of strain in relationships which occurs when the legitimate technical authority of the expert allows him to be judgemental in areas of family functioning over which he has no mandate.

What seems to be emerging in the literature on families is a stronger and stronger sense that professional-parental relationships are in urgent need of re-appraisal. The first is the appeal for professionals to acknowledge, by more than lip-service, that parents actually know a good deal about their child and that these insights and experiences are as valid and significant as professional judgements; that in the consultative process and in the decision processes, parents (and where possible the child himself) should be an active element and not a quiescent one. The second level is more revolutionary in that it seeks to see parents not only as recipients of services and advice, but as having (not simply the rights of partnership with professionals and a share in decisions) *the position and power to monitor and evaluate the effectiveness of professional services and intervention programmes.* Such power and influence are unlikely to accrue to individual sets of parents, and are much more likely to emerge from group pressure. These groups can

provide the parents with access to alternative information about services within the community, consultations with outside professionals, and moral support . . . viewed as isolated individuals few parents are likely to seem important enough to the average professional to have much influence on his future career. As members of a group of powerful parents' organizations, the parents' ability to influence the professional's career prospects is greatly enhanced . . . when the professional senses that his career depends as much upon parental satisfaction as it depends upon his relationship with his colleagues. (Gliedman and Roth, 1980: 170)

Of course, not all parents would be willing to give up the traditional relationship with professionals and are content with their passive-participatory role. Neither are all professional views of parents as over-reactive, over-protective or rejective simply explanatory devices to sustain a threatened ego, for there are families whose stress and anxiety necessitate support, counselling and therapy.

Professional-parental encounters

Professional-parental encounters are likely to be highly diverse but there are a few 'set-piece' encounters which figure prominently in the literature. These include the initial counselling following a birth defect; counselling and informing parents at some point in the child's development when a sensory, physical or mental handicap has become apparent; the hospitalized child; the child needing special schooling; and the decision to place the child in residential care. Though there is an excellent system for handling what might be called normal examples of exceptionality, the system is often put under strain when children are presented with unusual handicaps or multiple handicaps, which may involve territorial disputes between different specialisms or disciplines. As the *Court Report* (1976: 221) noted severe congenital abnormalities are usually recognized but it may take some time before non-visible disorders (like deafness or heart disease) are discovered, sometimes only revealing themselves as the child fails to acquire the skills and abilities normal for his age. The health service has been least successful in identifying the less severe disorders. In the past, but perhaps less so today, much effort was spent on correct classification of handicapped children. Arguments over whether this is a case of specific reading retardation or dyslexia, severe mental handicap or autism, and even where there is no diagnostic certainty the clutching at the 'Linus' blanket – minimal neurological dysfunctioning – often followed by a question mark are examples of potentially problematic cases. It is unfair to take any one case as typical of the encounters between parents and professionals and more valuable is the evidence that comes from interviews with parents, and where an observer has been present at a series of interviews.

In the latter case Strong (1979) has provided evidence of the qualitative nature of encounters between doctors and parents of a sick or handicapped child in a hospital setting. Alongside a wealth of transcripts of conversations, Strong focusses on ceremonial and ritual aspects of the interaction. Among the very many insights he offers we shall examine just a few. These encounters contain the potential for challenges to the parents' sense of moral worth. They may be seen and treated as good, indifferent or bad parents. Strong saw two styles of interactions at work here, face-work and character-work. 'Face-work' was where the identity of the parents and their moral worth were accepted as given, that is, if parents presented themselves as concerned, so they were treated. 'Character-work' might obtain when the professional explored the moral worth of the parent and attempted to change or reconstitute his or her character. 'Face-work' was more frequently observed. Indeed Strong suggests that one of the 'givens' in these encounters is an ideal perception of motherhood. Mothers were treated as serious and concerned, representing her children and their interests. From this basis of a given character the doctor was able to use a style which was gentle and calm. Mothers were perceived as open to self-criticism and willing to listen to advice. Doctors were calm, polite, serious, avoiding inconsistencies and eschewing character-work (except for failure to turn up for appointments).

Strong's interviews show medical staff to be understanding that the deepest of parental anxieties were the hardest to reveal. Questions were asked and answered over and over again to ensure agreement. This was another central feature of these encounters: the search for 'agreement'. This agreement occurred when parents and doctors were united in a common view of the child. Such an agreement might involve 'normalizing' the child (dispelling fears that were unfounded) or 'stigmatizing' the child (ensuring the parents understood the profound nature of their child's handicap). Where the intent was normalizing, doctors might use a 'search and destroy' technique – parents either on their own or with encouragement produced anxieties which the doctor calmed and demolished; parental ignorance was swiftly dispelled by medical expertise and vigorous attempts made to ensure that that view was accepted by parents.

But some interviews could not be based on 'search and destroy', and doctors had to handle the problem of informing parents of the gravest news. Here agreement was not so much sought as 'stalked', negotiated, 'luring towards acceptance' as Strong puts it. There was no assumption of easy agreement, the pace was slower and deliberate and doubts were amplified and not ignored. Strong saw doctors wanting to take time not only to gain a more accurate picture of the child but operating on the assumption that parents could not 'take it' in a single session.

Dr J.: She's a very nice mother. I think what we're trying to do is to introduce her very gradually to the fact that the child is very small, though we know the sort of child I mean. Well, we haven't really told the mother that. We've just said that she's going to be very small. Anyway she seems to be a candidate for delayed development and there's also this increased intra-cranial pressure, that's going to be a problem. Now at six months I saw her, that was at the special nursery follow-up clinic and she had a head-lag there, but of course then it wasn't necessarily developmental delay. So we saw her again at eight months, and by then she had got some head control but she hadn't her sitting balance. She had some hand movements and was vocalizing all right. So that seemed to be on the credit side. But at ten months we found that she wasn't sitting. The mother feels that otherwise she's doing all right there. She's not a very bright thing but I think in this case she's a pretty good judge of what the situation is. Then she was referred here. There has been this query about brain damage but we've not mentioned any of this to the mother. In fact the child had this very bashed-about head, she looked really awful when she was born.

This internal summary illustrates the filtering of data to the family and rather than giving the full data in one session the information was leaked over a long period.

The breaking of bad news was therefore an extremely delicate operation, in which staff probed to see how much parents suspected; produced some information and saw how they reacted; elaborated if they were challenged; withdrew slightly if the parents looked angry, and so on. Staff played a waiting game, not enforcing their own definition of a child but always leaving a part to be negotiated in each consultation, trying to build on last time's definition, but first waiting to see how parents commented on what had happened in the intervening weeks or months. As far as the two can be separated, the movement was from diagnosis to prognosis, first indicating what the child was and then saying what it would be. The movement from one to the other varied with the parents' receptiveness. No parent was told everything immediately, but some achieved detailed and dispassionate discussion far more quickly than others. (Strong, 1979: 124)

Although the impression gained from Strong's account is of professional concern and consideration, it is still true that the management of the encounter is organized around the professional's definition of the child and the process is towards acceptance of that definition, instantly or by degrees.

Such asymmetries of power, prestige and influence occur in many parental-professional encounters, in which parents experience not so much a sense of participation in decisions as being guided towards a predetermined view of their child. One study of eighty-two families explored relationships with health visitors, doctors and social workers and found that family responses to health visitors were positive in about half the families interviewed, a third neutral and a fifth negative. To doctors the responses were almost equally divided between positive and negative ones, while a similar image emerged with respect to social workers (Fox, 1974), but as he notes such statistics do not reveal anything like the complexity of relationships with professionals. One of the factors identified by Fox as contributing to communication difficulties was a lack of understanding by parents of the training, experience and competence of various professionals – for example, health visitors were not always identified as 'nurses' but were seen as 'motherly' rather than professional. There was uncertainty about the aims and motives of social workers, compounded with feelings of unease with young professionals from different social class backgrounds. General practitioners were seen as 'supportive' rather than interventionist, while hospital doctors were rated high on 'technology but low on humanity' (p. 62). But while these sociological abstractions like asymmetry of power and statistics of parental satisfactions with professional help are necessary to get a balanced picture they can become an anodyne to the real experience of family encounters with professionals. The following case is taken from Fox's transcripts.

'They get this training, but they don't really know how you feel'

Mrs B greeted me at the door of yet another small, externally uninviting terraced house. Inside, she and her husband had been hard at work; the outside lavatory had been incorporated into the house, the old yard replaced by a lavish kitchen, the front and back rooms united by a home-made archway. The furnishings were traditional, a blend of welcome and shabbiness. . . .

Mrs B was a spirited hostess, pressing me to tea and biscuits. She presented a curious amalgam of distinct nervousness with overt bonhomie, frankness and an enormous capacity for laughter, as well as a wry sense of humour which allowed her to view doctors and other professionals as though they shared roles in a comedy in addition to their burden of guilt. . . .

'I've always carried a chip on my shoulder since they first found out what was wrong with Kevin, his hypothyroidism. When he was six weeks old I detected that something wasn't quite right, and I took him back to the maternity ward where I had him; they told me he had hydrocephalus. The doctor just turned round to me and said, "We suspect hydrocephalus." Well I didn't know what hydrocephalus was. I thought he was just going to die in my arms . . . and I'd already lost one baby six months old, with a congenital heart. I thought, "My God, what is hydrocephalus?" you know, and I went home to my husband expecting him to die in the night. I went down to my own doctor the next morning and he told me what to expect. I was given an appointment at the Hydrocephalus Clinic, seeing terrible sights, for six months, and during that time they had him in, and investigated him, kept measuring his head which wasn't getting that much bigger, and at the end they gave him a lumbar puncture and said he didn't have any extra water and they couldn't see any signs of hydrocephalus. They said they didn't know what was wrong and they transferred me to the Endocrine Clinic. But while I was going up there I never saw the same doctor, which is another point I'd like to make. These different doctors, they all used to comment on the dryness of his skin, and his distended umbilical cord and all that, and I just – I was green, then, I didn't know what they were talking about – he went to the Endocrine Clinic and they used to say "Come back next month, it's just something you've got to live with, got to accept." But what I have to live with I just didn't know, it wasn't explained to me at all. I kept going back every month, month after month, I was sitting for hours and hours with little drops of milk in the bottle, Kevin was eleven months old but looked a little thing of five months, like a little ball of yellow fat, until one particular day I went up there and said I just couldn't carry on, I had another little boy of three who didn't know he had a mother and a husband who didn't know he had a wife. I was just screwing myself in corners, I didn't want to go out, I didn't want to wash myself, or anything: I just felt as though I had to keep grinning and trying to feed him. When I had my other boy, Mike, perfectly normal, I couldn't get rid of the welfare lady . . . they kept coming round, week after week, but when I had my Kevin I never saw a soul, on my life; and that was a time when I sorely needed somebody: I really thought I was going out of my mind. When you've lost one baby, it makes you feel a thousand times worse. I was sitting for hours just trying to feed him, and on this day when I went up there and said I couldn't carry on, you'll have to do something, either I'm going to leave home or I'll do something to myself, I told him, and I'll take the baby with me; so he said we'll have you and the baby in our annexe, and we'll learn you how to feed him. I thought you're not going to learn me in a fortnight what I've not learned in a year; I said, "He's my third baby, not my first," but I agreed to go in. I had to make arrangements with the almoner, she arranged that I would go up there, and when I got there I saw the admission doctor.

'He didn't even touch him! He just looked at him, and he was just a doctor, not a "mister somebody-or-other". He said to the nurse, "Are there any more notes on this baby, because I feel there should be? If your baby has got what I think he has, we've got a lot to be thankful for, because we'll be able to do

something for him," he said to me, "I think he's hypothyroid."
I thought to myself, "My God, something else." They never
explain something to you, that's what I like about doctors, they
never take the time to explain. I don't know whether they
think that you just ought to know all these long medical words.
Anyway, the matron of the Annexe found she couldn't feed the
baby at all, and she came to me and said, "We've got nothing to
learn you about feeding babies", and from that day nobody
came near me at the Annexe at feed times, I was just left
entirely by myself. For a few days they did these tests and it
was proven that he was hypothyroid. But why, oh why wasn't
it found out when I first took him up there when he was six
weeks old? . . . I shall never know. They should have gone
through these tests before. I saw another specialist after he was
put on thyroid tablets and he told me that owing to the fact that
he didn't have the thyroid from birth he had got a bit of brain
damage which could have been prevented if it had been found
out earlier. And that is what has made me so bitter. I don't
think they take enough time and trouble.'

She paused for the first time, shifted her position, gathered
my attention once more, and proceeded.

'I got a medical book out of the library, to find out what
hypothyroid meant. It stood out a mile. It all came back to me,
what the doctors had said when I was attending the Hydrocephalus Clinic: about the dryness of his skin, and the
yellowness of him, all the fluid under his skin. When I looked
back, I could only think how on earth it could have been
missed . . . I went to the Clinic to have him weighed, but that
was as far as it went, nobody used to bother to come around to
see me. I can't say I've got any help from anybody, once that
doctor knew what was wrong. He carried on under Mr G [she
mentioned a well-known paediatric endocrinologist], whom
he'd been seeing since he was six months old. Of course, when
he didn't find it out, and the admissions officer did, I lost all
confidence in him; I had none whatsoever at all, even up to
today. I've got no more confidence in that hospital . . . but I
still go for Kevin's sake. There's no one up there I can really
talk to. The almoners come and go.'

I asked her if she had been to the Clinic.

'I got past it. I thought, if they're not going to worry, then why should I? It just used to annoy me to think that nobody came round. As I'd never had much to do with the Clinic — when I went down there with my first baby, everything seemed to be so secretive. They don't tell you anything, and I hate to be treated as though I'm ignorant. This is the whole crux of the matter. When I used to go to the Children's Hospital nine times out of ten Mr G would have students sitting with him, and I well remember one particular time when I took Kevin up there . . . I noticed one side of his face seemed to be different to the other, and I happened to mention this . . . you do, you try to tell them every little thing that's worrying you. When I told this to Mr G, one of these young fellows started laughing, he sort of looked around at the others, grinning, as though I'd said something stupid. I felt about as big as that. I just gave him a terrible look . . . if looks could've killed he'd have dropped dead, and I just shut up.

'I'd have liked somebody to be visiting me, knowing how I felt, but I wouldn't have liked someone in authority. What gets me is the almoners: they've not had any children . . . I know they get this training, but they don't really know how you feel' (Fox, 1974: 10–16)

McCormack (1978) suggests that between parents and professionals there is a gulf, 'a feeling that with the best training and the best will in the world professionals cannot really understand the child and his problems', while professionals see parents as emotive and lacking in realism. McCormack describes a scene at a special school where before an audience of parents the head teacher described the school as a nucleus of help surrounded by a multi-disciplinary team.

There was hollow laughter from parents of older children who have attempted to call upon such services, for years — and found them not forthcoming or not helpful. One mother had been waiting nine months for an appointment with an educational psychologist: another had been lucky enough to see one, with disappointing results. 'You'll find he has a set number of problems on his list and the answers beside them. If your child does not fit one of his pigeon-holes, he doesn't know what to do,' she insisted. (McCormack, 1978: 183)

Special schools and their teachers are often more integrated into parental relationships than are relationships with doctor or social workers.

There are several valuable accounts of family involvement with professionals. Among the ones particularly recommended are Elizabeth Browning's *I Can't See What You're Saying* (1972) and *The Seige* by C.C. Park (1967). Mrs Browning's story concerns Freddy, a boy who consistently fell through the net of services through failure to fit neatly into existing professional pigeon-holes. It is also a reminder that changes in patterns of services are often instigated by one determined individual, and that if you happen to be born with a rare handicap do try to choose a determined and vigorous parent quite prepared to challenge bureaucratic decisions.

Freddy, by eighteen months, had not begun to talk and his family took him to their GP who thought his ear-drums might be blocked, sent him on to an ENT specialist – 'processing children like a conveyor belt' – who said there was nothing wrong with his ear-drums so he must be deaf so go and see Professor X, and next please. Seeing the specialist resulted in the verdict that the child was not deaf and was intelligent. By three years of age a further expert examination produced the verdict that if he did not talk by three-and-a-half years he never would. The next specialist informed them that Freddy was a 'straightforward case of aphasia'. After a good deal of searching a special school was found and after a settling-in period his parents were informed he was ready for normal schooling (although he was very backward educationally), and his parents were stunned by this news.

> Out of the blue we had been informed by post that he was fit for normal education and should leave by the end of the summer term . . . When we arrived [at the school] we were shown into a room with a large dining table and chairs and no one suggested we sat down. The principal came in and we prepared to ask our questions about Freddy's future. She stated loud and clear that his speech had improved so much while at the school that he was quite ready for normal school. His speech in fact was not good even if it was a lot better than that of some of the other children. We pointed out that he could not do sums, still could not read, could barely write and still had a gross comprehen-

sion problem . . . I asked the principal how she thought he would get on in a secondary school in a large class unable to read. My question was ignored . . . Suddenly the principal left the room leaving the door wide open and we both thought she had gone to fetch a file or one of the teachers. We waited. We waited longer. We waited longer still and then it slowly dawned upon us that, unbelievably, we had had our answer. (Browning, 1972: 57–8)

Mrs Browning acknowledges that she encountered superb clinical expertise but all too infrequently sympathy and understanding. She has a nice expression to convey her feelings about bureaucrats shackled by their own red tape when she felt like 'swinging her handbag' – some of them did not know how close they came to receiving it. But it is never swung. Parents know their behaviour is as much under scrutiny as their child's, and direct confrontations with authority require great courage or are the product of desperation. Meekness may be an effective tactic, but occasionally more abrasive methods are rewarding. A case reported in *The Observer* (1 October 1978) drew attention to children in one family mistakenly diagnosed as clumsy and subnormal who were in fact suffering from a rare visual defect. Only the persistence of the family produced the correct diagnosis.

The vulnerability of parents to the victim-blaming syndrome is one of the dominant themes in contemporary literature on families with a handicapped child. It has become all too frequent to find in parental 'attitudes' an explanation for the child's problems. Such a perspective can be especially destructive when expert opinion believes that the handicap is related to family psychopathology. The next example comes from a family with an autistic child and illustrates both the positive and negative sides of parent-professional involvement.

Mrs C.C. Park has described in *The Siege* (1967) some of her encounters on the road to obtaining help for her autistic child, Elly. At three-and-a-half years Elly was taken for an examination to a clinic. The Institute wished to do a thorough job of diagnosis and assessment, and this included observation of the child and interviews with the parents, which would take about ten days. Such arrangements are not easy for a family to make and they requested a delay to make the necessary arrangements. In the absence of letters a telephone call was made and an appointment was made in three days. Luckily they were able to sort their domestic affairs. Mrs Park writes:

> We were learning what we could have guessed: that the Institute although theoretically aware that human beings exist in social contexts – that their family life is complicated – was not interested in visualizing any detail of the life that went on outside their large, comfortable building. They had no concern with the difficulties of providing for our children in the longest absence from home we had ever had. They had scarcely more interest in what we were to do with Elly during our first interview. We learned with astonishment that we were not to bring her. Not to bring her? Where could we leave her? Surely in so well-staffed an institution there were people with whom she could stay while my husband and I were interviewed? Apparently not. It was not their practice to allow parents to bring the child on the first interview. (Park, 1967: 131)

The parents were seen separately; then Elly was seen by the psychiatrist: an intelligence test was administered, she was observed in a nursery school, and was given a neurological examination. The interviews were not like tutorials at a university where two or three people are together in a room, exchanging views, with one knowledgeable person leading the discussion, a situation familiar to both Mr and Mrs Park.

> We were consequently slow to realize that the whole method of these interviews was so set up as to eliminate any possibility of a natural relationship between the two people in the room. The method was simple but rigid. We were not there to consult but to talk – to talk steadily, without guidance, without response, to an almost totally passive listener who was studiously careful to betray no reaction and volunteer no information. (ibid.: 132)

A difficult enough situation for anyone but especially so for a parent seeking help. Natural conversation was difficult and the obvious social tactic was to be 'reasonable and obedient'.
'I began to take out the material I had brought – the photographs that showed the progress of the condition from babyhood, the notebooks recording skills, vocabulary, the games we played.' There were offered as a means of contact. They were

not wanted; it was not their practice. It became a guessing game – what did they want, for questions were avoided? After a month and a half the verdict was given. Here it is, complete and unabridged. 1) Elly needed psychotherapy, 2) she had performed above her age level on the part of the IQ test she could do and it was their belief that she had no mental deficiency, 3) she had many fears. They had read the notebooks and found them very interesting. No further help was offered. The Parks responded nobly to this – they laughed, at first, saying it was

> only gradually that we began to feel angry and resentful, to react as intelligent adults, not obedient children in the hands of those wiser than we. Our powers of indignation reawakened . . . indignation at this pleasant, passive, blandly inconsiderate institution. (ibid.: 131)

Mrs Park has this to say about her experience.

> Comfortable, well-educated members of the upper middle class ordinarily escape the experience of de-personalization, of either helplessness in institutional hands, of reduction to the status of children to whom situations are mediated, not explained. Like so much that hurts the experience is deeply educative. We know now in ourselves that the most threatening of all attacks is the attack on the sense of personal worth, that the harshest of all deprivations is the deprivation of respect. We know now, I think, how the slum mother feels when the welfare worker comes round the corner. It takes, one would think, so little knowledge of psychology, to put oneself in someone else's place. (ibid.: 139)

The formal cold face of officialdom is frightening, baffling and capable of arousing despair. Mrs Browning writes of the power of people in power: 'Thoughts as sharp as needles were sparkling through my head, thoughts about power and people: destinies in the hands of others. Kafka made real,' for 'Circumstances alter, people never' (ibid.: 66).

Mrs Park brought Elly to Anna Freud's clinic in Hampstead. More interviews and examinations here but in a quite different atmosphere. Conversation was more natural, unforced, jokes allowed, questions permitted, the notebooks read, mother and child were observed playing together and the final accolade, the social worker saying 'I think we can learn something from you'. The diagnosis suggested that Elly was unlikely to suffer a massive regression. 'One is less vulnerable to pain than to understanding and kindness. One develops defences against slights or insensitivity: against kindness, none.'

Partnership

There is one area in which the concept of partnership between professionals and parents has developed some way beyond mere rhetoric: this is in the field of mental handicap. Mittler (1979) has described the growth and development of practical courses (workshops and child development programmes) but rather more than a simple transfer of skills seems to be taking place. What is happening is nothing short of a re-evaluation of professional attitudes which is not only recognizing that parents have an important role to play in backing up the programme of the special or mainstream school, but that they are regarded as knowledgeable, expert and contributory partners in planning and implementing programmes. They are also seen as having an evaluating role in considering professional contributions. While there is some doubt as to the extent to which the value position of partnership has been translated into reality, we have nothing like the degree of commitment to parents that can be found in America under Public Law 94–142, the Education for All Handicapped Children, 1975. Such a significant re-thinking of parental-professional relationships we may regard as a potentially rich model for extension into other areas, but until the role of parents and their rights become more structured into the philosophy and practice of care agencies it will still be necessary for them to be vigorous and combative to get the best out of the system for their child.

Summary

Few families with a disabled or handicapped child can meet the child's needs without help from outside the family. This help may be financial, or offers of advice on management and care, personal counselling, and educational and medical services, and many others. Through their contacts with various professional agencies, parents may well find that their own definition of their child conflicts with that offered by professionals and there are differing views as to whether parents' views are significantly shaped by professional definitions or whether they are able to sustain their own. While there is an almost bewildering array of services, both State and voluntary, on which parents may call, it is the experience of many families that access to such services depends upon their skill and tenacity. In the accounts provided by parents it appears they are conscious of an asymmetry of power between themselves and the agencies which exist to serve them. There is emerging a stronger belief that parents should be regarded not only as valued resources with unmatched knowledge of their children but that they have a right to monitor and evaluate the effectiveness of the services provided for them.

8
Public experiences and private feelings

Deviance is a form of social differentiation which is not always confined to the person singled out but spreads to those in close contact with him. Individuals who are perceived as deviant may find their stigma rippling outwards to affect persons who are associated with them, who may be regarded as being given a courtesy stigma by virtue of their association. However, this brand is not visible and such courtesy stigma if applied may be restricted to those occasions when they are in the presence of the stigmatized person and so courtesy stigmata are a situationally induced phenomenon. This construct of a courtesy stigma has been applied to families with a handicapped child.

Among families with a disabled or handicapped child, the situational variability of a courtesy stigma is clear. The child's father may be 'taint' free at his place of work, and parents will be undifferentiated when out together at a cinema or spending an evening with friends. At home among considerate family or friends the social context may minimize or avoid imputations of shared deviance. But in public places with the child parents are more vulnerable to others' definition of them and their offspring. Also the care and educational needs of the child expose the family to judgements by a variety of professionals. Since parental definitions of their child are to some extent shaped by how others react to them and their child, whether in public places or in private consultations, the whole complex of inter-personal perception and behaviour becomes an important facet of the experience of handicap.

The family may have worked through their own feelings about having a handicapped child, but moving out from the security of the home into the more exposed public domain can threaten that fragile acceptance. The evidence from parents and from re-searchers presents an inconsistent picture of family-community ranging from concerned and sympathetic understanding to downright rudeness and hostility. Equally varied are the reports of the range of parental responses to their public reception from toughminded abrasiveness to timid and shrinking reluctance to move from the security of family and considerate friends. Darling (1979) shows something of the variability of parental attitudes with accounts of parents of children with spina bifida where in one study parents reported they were not abashed at people knowing about their child's handicap and generally found them helpful and understanding, while in another study of a similar parental group it was found that parents were often disconcerted by the remarks and glances of others. A third study of parents with children with cystic fibrosis was almost equally split between those who found the community helpful and positive, and those who felt the reverse. The extent to which these views are objective is impossible to determine. Perceptions of community isolation may be related to parents' personalities but such perceptions are completely valid for each parent.

Woodburn (1972) in her study of spina bifida found about a third of families found their child had restricted their social contacts, but some experienced a growth of social relationships mainly through having a friendly and outgoing child who encouraged conversations with neighbours and strangers. Among her sample there were some who felt 'cut-off emotionally' and 'different from other people' (p. 240) and had to deal with morbid curiosity and even hostility, although the general impression was of helpfulness. What came through very clearly is that mothers felt confident in being able to distinguish between genuine and counterfeit sympathy, although dealing with it was often problematic. As well as expressions of concern, there were also comments from strangers who offered unsolicited such observations as 'You should put that child in a home' (p. 243), and to a disabled child 'Time you were on your feet, my lad' (p. 244). Following such shattering bluntness mothers were enraged or upset and became liable to be apprehensive about subsequent public experiences.

Gregory (1976) shows how the invisible handicap of deafness in a child has a positive advantage in that the child looks normal but also the disadvantage of creating misunderstanding since the child's behaviour is thought due to inadequate parental control, and parents are not able to explain the problems very easily to strangers. Gregory suggests that parents of deaf children can help to make society more aware of the problems of the normal-looking handicapped child, although she notes that the cultural context of English society makes mentioning a child's handicap an act of nosiness or intrusiveness, while equally, awkwardness and unease can occur when neighbours never mention the handicap.

Voysey (1975) found that parents of disabled children develop and use a variety of ways of creating the 'right' impression of their child and of their role as parents. This is not a skill reserved for parents of handicapped children since all parents like their children to be seen in a good light which reflects back on them. For Voysey the essential goal of impression management 'is to create an image of a normal child in which the cast (parents and child together) engage in preparatory "backstage" work to produce the effect'. This may be in the use of clothing or other props to minimize the visibility of the handicap or other kinds of information control, such as not revealing the true age of the child, and through the course of many encounters, parents learn to be skilled role makers. While minimizing the handicap may be one form of impression management there are occasions when the presentation of the child requires emphasizing or even exaggerating the handicap. I once interviewed a number of parents of autistic children seeking to place their child in a residential school and one aspect that emerged clearly was the ambiguity of their perceptions of how to 'present' their child – presented as too handicapped and the chance of a place would be lost; while presented as not handicapped enough might have the same result.

The management of self and child in exposed settings can be problematic, for since children – especially young ones – are somewhat unreliable performers (and handicapped children may be extremely unreliable) they threaten the preferred parental definition. The mother whose brain-damaged child runs amok in a crowded supermarket may find her control over the presentation of her child and herself totally wrecked. As Birenbaum (1971) has noted, one way of coping with vulnerability is for parents to circumscribe their environment and relationships by keeping to a narrow circle of understanding relatives and considerate friends. It must be a matter of speculation how far family isolation is determined by negative social experiences, but it is likely to play a significant part unless countered by a strong determination not to be cowed.

In John and Eileen Wilks' book *Bernard: Bringing up our Mongol Son* (1974) we find a sensitive and sensible account of the process by which one set of parents grew from uncertainty to a measure of confidence in their capacity to cope both with their child and the community.

> One of the things which we found most difficult was to talk about him to other people and to deal with situations in which he became involved with other people. (Wilks, 1974: 34)

Like many other mothers, in the beginning Mrs Wilks found it difficult to talk about Bernard without becoming upset. One of her private tactics was not to think too much about his condition, taking each day as it came along and keeping many of the daily difficulties to herself. Learning to talk to other people was a slow process with skills built up over many years, but gradually she was able to talk about him without becoming emotional, and was no longer anxious just thinking about him. However, simple everyday occurrences could upset this calm. Walking along with Bernard and a younger brother, two ladies remarked on 'what a fine pair of twins' they were – when they looked closely at Bernard their expression changed. Mrs Wilks learned to cope with the stares and backward glances and gained enough confidence to take him about with her, but as he grew older his behaviour became more noticeable and he went through a 'naughty phase' from four to ten years (some phase).

They write,

> We recently saw a pamphlet about the mentally handicapped which included the advice: 'You can recognize that mental handicap is a normal occurrence in any community in the world. You can show your acceptance of that by being neither over-curious nor under-interested in the handicapped person and his family.' This is sound advice, but if one pauses for a moment, one sees that there is a very delicate dividing line between being over-curious and under-interested. Not surprisingly both Eileen and I felt that some reactions to Bernard fell into one or other of these categories. (ibid.: 36–7)

Mrs Wilks suggests that 'One always finds it easy to talk

naturally to parents who themselves have a child who is handicapped in some way.' Mary Craig (1979: 142) takes a similar view of how in distress we intuitively seek out a friend who has experienced sorrow rather than one whose path has always been smooth. John and Eileen Wilks again:

> Just as people find it difficult to talk to parents, so they find it difficult to behave naturally with handicapped children. Many people speak to them quite differently from the way they speak to normal children – such as giving them a friendly pat on the head. (ibid.: 40)

Sometimes people were much more friendly to Bernard than to other children. 'They would joke with him, tease him, and slap him on the back.'

Van der Hoeven, writing about bringing up a boy with Down's Syndrome in Holland, has this to say:

> There is something about our nation that is fascinated by illness and everything connected with it. It has to be discussed with relish and preferably at great length. My wife stood in the shop and heard someone remark, 'What a poor lamb.' Another confirmed this by saying, 'Dreadful, isn't it.' She looked at Aat's censors and told them that though it might seem dreadful Aat was none the less a very sweet child and a very happy one. It was a poor defence. (Hoeven, 1968: 113)

As Mrs Wilks noted, conversations between parents with handicapped children are seen as 'natural' and unforced. Common meeting points, such as special schools, clinics and hospitals, may make such contacts easier. Birenbaum (1971) found that while informal association was refreshing and helpful it did not lead to the establishment of close friendships.

> Friendships with others who are stigmatized do not support a normal appearing round of life, since they can be mis-interpreted by others as a general identification with one's fate. In general mothers regard participation in the organized world of mental retardation to be specifically for the child. (Birenbaum, 1971: 201)

While some mothers may retreat into a self-chosen world of considerate friends, others take a more robust stance, toughened by careless or thoughtless behaviour, and able to shrug off or ignore such behaviour.

It is to be hoped that, with greater awareness by the public through the impact of television and other sources of mass communication, the interactional awkwardness of parents with disabled children will be lessened simply through the greater availability of positive images of children and parents. Also, as has already been mentioned in the case of deafness, there is an important role for parents to play with respect to dispelling ignorance, but the central problem is that in our everyday social repertoire there is no easy interactional model to determine an effective way of responding.

Separation

A great deal of what we have been considering concerns the intact family. For families with handicapped children, family unity can be disturbed by various forms of separation. Roskies (1972) noted that mothers of thalidomide-damaged babies were kept apart from their child for several days after the child's birth and she speculated whether this separation at a crucial stage of mother-child bonding, might have serious consequences for subsequent attachment. Children with medical or surgical problems can require lengthy and frequent periods of hospital treatment – for example one child with spina bifida required thirty periods in hospital between birth and ten years of age. Other children may require 'five day' boarding provision or full-time residential provision. Parents of mentally handicapped children may look for short-term care for their child as a measure of relief from the constant burden of care, and then there are the children who are permanently separated from their families in institutional care.

Bowlby (1969) argued that 'attachment behaviour' is a pattern of behaviour the goal of which is to maintain a set of relationships between mother and child which maximizes the likelihood of the child's survival. Attachment behaviour may be threatened by events like hospitalization. With increasing age children appear to develop a greater tolerance for separation but this is at its lowest in very young children, and while brief separation can be managed without serious psychological consequences, prolonged separation can have damaging effects on the developing personality. The distress of young children in hospital has been noted by many commentators with its 'protest', 'despair' and finally 'detachment', so the negative effects of hospitalization increase with lengthy stays and how far the child has gone along the protest-despair-detachment road. While modern research (Hall, 1979) has found that children experience a 'discontinuity' of relationships when placed in hospital, their reaction to that experience varies with family and temperamental characteristics and that long-term personality changes are not an invariable feature of separation. Nevertheless, the experience of separation is seldom easy to manage for either parent or child. Pill (1979: 143) in a study of hospitalized, handicapped children argues that the family's view of the child and the purpose of hospitalization need to be considered in understanding the impact of separation. It was found that severely handicapped children run the risk of becoming long-stay patients through the factors which are associated with admission. Visiting is a greater financial burden on low-income families and the desire to visit may be attenuated if parents are unconsciously contemplating institutional placement. It is also thought that such a context enables professionals to form a judgement that the family is 'incapable' of providing for the child and a path to institutional care is more clearly seen as a management option.

The theme of separation runs through the experiences of many families especially those with children requiring scarce forms of treatment. It is administratively simpler to collect these scarce resources in regional centres and to bring children to them rather than taking the services out to the community. Parents may have the torment in abundance of knowing the psychological cost to themselves and their child of family separation, while to keep him at home may deprive him of much needed services. Mrs Browning, whose book about Freddy the boy with asphasia has already been mentioned, describes this parental conflict when after a great struggle she finally secured a place for Freddy in a residential school: the parting from her child was nevertheless harrowing. While there is much evidence on the disadvantages of residential special schooling, Rackham (1975) presents a case for the residential school caring for children with asthma, diabetes and epilepsy where skilled round-the-clock care and observation can take place and treatment given in an unemotional way. One of her justifications for such provision is where family stress is part of the clinical picture. Not all parents are reluctant to send their children away and for some this may be essential to their mental and physical health, so the rationale for placement is in the best interest of the family not just the child, and there are a few who simply use institutional provision as a convenient off-loading facility.

The bleaker side of institutional life for mentally handicapped children has been ably recorded by Oswin (1971) and for the physically handicapped by Miller and Gwynne (1972), but as Tizard and Tizard (1974) have shown, it is possible for institutions to overcome many of their inherent disadvantages and become centres for the development of children's potential. For parents who place their child in a residential school or 'total' institution for anything but the most negative of motives, the decision to part with their child is often difficult and seldom arrived at or followed through without moments of reflection over the right-ness of such an apparently irrevocable step.

As an example of the ambiguity, uncertainty and emotional pressure under which these decisions are taken, we have a short extract from Nel and Peter Motte's *The Hand of the Potter* (1956) in which they record their experiences in diary form. Here Peter Motte writes of his feelings once they had decided to place their son Richard in an institution, because of his violent and potentially self-destructive behaviour.

So Richard was to live away from us forever. This time I didn't feel the same at all. I don't know why. Before I had missed him more than I would have thought possible: now his absence seems the most natural thing in the world. Perhaps I had realized how much Nel meant to me, and that Richard was not only claiming time, energy and thought that should have been for me, but was ruining Nel's health. Perhaps subconsciously I realized that I was making my choice between Richard and Nel and having chosen was determined to put Richard out of my mind. For I did have to choose. It was a tragic and dreadful choice, but it had to be made. And how could I choose differently. Nel, for nearly twenty years, had been most of my life. Richard could never be more than a burden and an anxiety and one day would have to go to strangers, for if either of us died, the other could not have carried on with him for a week. Better to make the break now, while we had each other. Did I make the wrong choice? . . .

We were invited to see the quarters where Richard would spend probably the rest of his life . . . the children were crowded into one room (other rooms were being redecorated), the doctor opened the door – they were sitting around the wall, some on benches some on the floor. One was rocking to and fro . . .

Such children fifty years ago had little hope of surviving more than twelve or thirteen years. Chest complaints were the usual cause of death. Today, [with] the rapid progress in new remedies . . . their expectation of life has been increased to twenty, and before Richard is twenty it will probably have increased much further. But the question remains, have we done right? . . . if you could have seen him that day before Christmas with his head bruised and bleeding from self-injury, you would have instantly agreed that he was beyond everything except skilled nursing and constant expert supervision. . . .

We sought and found the best advice in the country . . . the decision was unanimous – 'You have no right to keep him with you.' (Motte, 1956: 88–97)

While parents, and they are the majority, are able to manage difficult and demanding children, with increasing age even the most willing can find themselves becoming progressively preoccupied with questions about the long-term care of their child. Margaret Brock's *Christopher* (1975) records some twenty-seven years of love and concern for her deaf and blind son. It was a very close, happy and rewarding relationship, but one which had placed many restrictions and constrictions on her personal and social life, and now the moment had arrived when this loving relationship was being changed through a decision to find a permanent residential home for him.

I know what we should do, before we begin to resent the many social deprivations Christopher causes us. I know too that he would settle down well and happily anywhere where there were kind and gentle people with time to think about him and help him into a new life and it will be me who will be lost and devastated, free for the first time of twenty-seven years' full-time responsibility, needing him more than he needs me. It seems such a repudiation of all we have tried to give him over the years, to send him away now, but I think we have come to the place of acceptance at last . . . We have tried and now perhaps we have accepted that this is the time for someone else to try and enrich the rest of his life. (Brock, 1975: 122)

While there is much concern for the family with a young handicapped child, and the stress on young parents and normal siblings, the circumstances of older parents caring for their grown disabled children is equally difficult. Something of the constant care emerges in Archie Hill's *Closed World of Love* (1976), a superbly written account of family relationships. In this brief excerpt he manages to convey the physical and emotional drain on one mother.

He has messed himself. I can smell it. We clean and change him . . . she has been doing this for twenty-seven years, my wife. Simple arithmetic tells me she has changed over thirty thousand nappies for him – each one has to be slightly more than a few feet long . . . she's changed twelve miles of nappies for her son. . . .
We talcum his buttocks and groin. A safe, sweet family smell, Woolworth's smell. His dark haired head on the pillow. As it turns, I see a glimpse of me and here and there a ghost of his mother, a sigh and a promise of her, a quickened likeness that appears and is gone. From the corner of my eye I watch his mother – so beautiful when I met her, so lively, so full of pure life. Faded now and tired, a tired monument to sacrifice. (Hill, 1976: 97–8)

Although the picture drawn by Hill is authentic for families with a severely handicapped child who requires constant care and attention it needs to be contrasted with the many hundreds of families where life with a disabled child has been as happy and contented as could be wished; where the child has added to family cohesiveness, where parents have found satisfaction in ensuring the child's place in the mainstream of schooling and of life in general, and where they have been able to encourage greater independence and achievement, and have helped to open up many opportunities. It is also the case that even where independent, integrated living has not been achieved by the child many families have been able to develop a style of living which is mutually enhancing.

Terminal illness

Childhood deaths from pneumonia, tuberculosis and diphtheria, the killers of earlier generations, are now very rare occurrences in this country but there are the sudden and not well understood deaths of infants (cot deaths) as well as fatalities from accidents. Leukaemia, progressive disorders of muscles and nervous system, and brain tumours also take their toll. Cystic fibrosis with its repeated chest infections is another example of a condition where treatment can prolong life but in which there is a mortality risk to children. Duchenne muscular dystrophy, 'inexorable in progress and fatal in outcome' (Dodge, 1974: 12), with its progressive effects on mobility is a condition in which intelligence is unaffected and the child may be fully aware of the prognosis especially if he has had similarly affected older brothers.

For the handicapped child with a terminal condition, all who are involved in his treatment and education, as well as his immediate family, will be caught up in the emotional impact of the situation. Oswin (1974: 114) notes that the teacher is faced with the least difficult role – unlike the nurse she does not have to give painful treatment, unlike the doctor she does not have to take decisions over surgery or treatment. Unlike the physiotherapist she is not called upon to make physical demands on the child, nor is she called upon to comfort and counsel grieving parents like the social worker. But Oswin provides numerous examples of how the teacher in a hospital or special school can be supportive of the child, and have a concern for other children and for colleagues. Yvonne Craig in Burton's *The Care of the Dying Child* (1974) has described the stress on her family of the care of her daughter Claire who had leukaemia. Such accounts are painful to read, hard to write and almost unbearable to experience. While there is not the space here to develop the theme of the role of professionals in responding to this extreme form of family crisis it would not have been appropriate to ignore totally this aspect of the experience of handicap.

Summary

Parents of handicapped children are particularly vulnerable in the company of their child to the reactions of other people. There is evidence that parents' reception in the community is varied, some finding the community supportive and helpful and others the opposite. It has been suggested that some families find the management of community responses problematic and this leads to a restriction of social activities to the home and considerate friends. The requirement of families to interact with a variety of agencies has led some writers to suggest they develop impression management strategies. Among the parents whose experiences were drawn upon we find examples of the difficulties parents can experience in encounters with the community and just how delicate is the divide between over-curiosity and under-involvement. Perhaps more significant is the issue of separation which is frequently the case with children who require repeated hospitalization or residential care. Even when families are supportive and caring for the child, when that child grows to be an adult they may be forced to consider a permanent form of separation.

9

Childhood with a disability

Childhood is never an easy period to recall and apart from a few highly gifted professionals like Virginia Axline and Bruno Bettelheim, the reconstruction of childhood has been the province of the writer rather than the child psychologist who has the power to create a sense of a world being seen and experienced by children.

Vivid and total recall of childhood is not readily available and perhaps more commonplace is that of adults looking back, which does not have the advantage of a continuous narrative but possesses a disjointed, fragmented and unorganized perception of childhood – not a cine-film, but a series of snapshots – and even these may have been carefully edited. We may derive a partial understanding through observation of children, the study of their unfolding abilities, the development of their personality and growth towards adult status, yet this compartmentalization so often increases the distance between us and them as complicated beings with a distinctive view of the world. One might almost go so far as to say that what is missing from many books on child development is childhood, and that it is to autobiography and fiction that we turn to see the fragments re-assembled.

The childhood of those who were disabled has a double significance because these sources are comparatively few in number and they provide a rare opportunity for us to attempt some imaginative bridge-building between their experiences and our own. As professionals we need to try to appreciate not only the part of the whole child that is our particular professional concern but also how the child appears to see us and what we are doing to or for him.

Of the principle themes of a handicapped childhood, I would select the following as being centrally significant: relationships within the family, the experience of hospitalization, treatment, schooling, awareness of handicap and adolescence. It is believed that the way a child adapts to his disability is largely shaped by the attitudes he first encounters in the home. Eileen Scott writing about bringing up a blind child remarks: 'What every visually handicapped child needs most is a set of parents who are intelligent, emotionally mature, socially competent, financially secure, and just crazy about small children' (Scott, 1979: 81). Which would be rather a good recipe for all children.

Relatively few studies have explored disabled children's perceptions of their family relationships. One early study (Cruickshank, 1952) examined this aspect through a series of sentence-completion tasks. As well as examining children's attitudes to peer groups, society and disabled people, the study sought data on children's views and feelings about their parents. The replies to sentences containing the word 'father' indicated that there were both positive and negative feelings towards fathers in the disabled group. Compared to a control group of normal children, disabled children used more neutral responses to the stimulus word and the control group used both stronger positive and stronger negative responses than did the disabled group. Cruickshank suggests that this indicates that the disabled group was less able to evaluate their relationship with their father than control group subjects.

Both groups gave a high percentage of positive responses to the sentences containing the stimulus word 'mother'. Both groups gave approximately the same degree of positive and negative responses, and Cruickshank indicates that there was evidence that the disabled group felt sufficiently secure in their relation-ship with their mother to be critical of her. In their relationship with her these disabled children were 'more accurate and more mature in evaluation of feelings' than towards their father. On the whole disabled children showed a more positive relationship with the mother than the father compared to normal children. On 'family' sentences the disabled child showed both a stronger feeling for the security of a place within the home but also greater anxiety about 'family activities' and this is thought to indicate some measure of uncertainty about his role within the family which becomes more acute when the family do things together. In his summary of the research Cruickshank draws attention to the following:

1) disabled children have generally better relationships with mother than father,
2) have a greater dissatisfaction with adults and adult society than do non-handicapped children,
3) express a greater desire to be treated like other children rather than children with a handicap,
4) have greater difficulties in evaluating interpersonal relationships,
5) show a greater tendency to withdraw from social contacts,
6) have a narrower range of interests,
7) and how they perceive the impact of their handicap is impressed on them more by adults then by their peer group. (Cruickshank, 1952: 109)

The hospitalization of disabled children is usually discussed in terms of separation and deprivation but, as Hall and Stacey (1979) have shown, hospital involves the child not only in the stress of separation from his family, but also the learning of a new role and the formation of a new set of relationships. Davis (1956), on the hospital experience of children with polio, wrote:

In a very real sense he is thrown into an entirely new world from the one to which he is accustomed. The paralysis affects not only his ability to manipulate his own body but also severely alters his customary motor relations with significant others and social objects. In a great many cases he cannot walk for several months following an acute attack. He is taken away from family and playmates and set down in strange surroundings where the routine is unfamiliar . . . He is one among many [children]. Generally he has only the vaguest idea of what is being done to him or why it is being done. (Davis, 1956, i Filstead, 1973: 114)

Davis comments on the restructuring of time for patients who are hospitalized and who learn the role as a co-operative patient (one who doesn't whine for home) as well as the moral implication of tapping and using 'willpower' in the rehabilitation process – what he calls the quintessence of Protestant ideology – 'slow, patient and regularly applied effort in pursuit of long-term goals' (p. 116). Hospital régime and treatment programmes are not simply medical activities, they involve roles and moral judgements. (See also Polly Toynbee's *Hospital* (1977).)

Schooling, whether special or mainstream, marks out a distinctive phase in the career of a disabled child. It can be the beginning of a life-long process of stigmatization or a stage in the process of normalization. Special schooling with others similarly handicapped can be an emotional shock to a handicapped child when he realizes that his condition is not necessarily remediable. Minde (1972), in his study of disabled pupils at a special school, saw them growing through several phases – disorientation through loss of home links, depression as a more realistic view of their physical status was brought home by contact with older pupils with similar impairments which had not been miraculously cured, and a period of pre-adolescent revolt settling back into a state of acceptance. During this period there was a growing sense of awareness of being different from able-bodied peers, and like all children the disabled and handicapped are especially vulnerable during adolescence, but perhaps the disabled are more unsettled since at this time together with leaving school, they often become critically aware of the possibilities of the future and the limits which their disabilities and society impose upon their performance of a full complement of adult roles.

Adolescence is an especially difficult phase in most children's development and it may be that this period contains additional difficulties for the young person who is disabled. Perhaps this is the time at which they come to see for the first time the shape of their life to come. Differences between themselves and able-bodied peers are perceived with a new clarity and a number of researches have shown this phase to be one where the disabled young person begins to question the meaning of his life and where an indefinite future which has to incorporate his disability becomes a reality.

Some examples from a handicapped childhood

I've always been attracted to Vera Dean's autobiography *Three Steps Forward* (1957) in which she describes, laconically, a childhood crippled by spasticity. From this rich source I've chosen a brief extract from her first day in hospital. Hospital treatment is very much part of the childhood experience of disabled children. We know a good deal about the dangers that separation of the mother and child can hold and something of the trauma of hospitalization, with its strange routines and its fears and pain. Undoubtedly things have changed in children's hospitals since Vera Dean's days, but for the child newly admitted the situation is basically unaltered. Vera Dean was admitted to hospital when she was twelve and put to bed on her arrival. She tried to talk to other children in the ward but couldn't communicate because of her speech defect. Like Denton Welch, she experienced the uncertainty of not knowing what was happening to her. She was kept in bed for a month, then allowed up in a wheelchair but not permitted to take part in 'school'.

> After a month of just sitting in bed I was allowed to get up. We all got up at 5.30 to give us time to dress for breakfast at eight. . . .
>
> Breakfast, dinner or tea it made no difference. Bibs were put on us but there were not enough nurses to feed us all so we had to feed ourselves and the food went everywhere. When we did not like our food it would go on the floor or the ceiling. . . . [Lessons were difficult, she did not have a suitable desk and she dribbled on her work.] One day, she [the teacher] told the class to write out the well-known poem 'Trees'. I thought that if I wrote this all right she would mark it and be pleased. It took me a month to do and it was very hard work which I did not enjoy. Every day I hung the bit I had done over the fireguard to dry – it was so wet with dribble. When I finished the teacher did not mark it because she couldn't understand my scribble. I was so hurt that I did not worry about school for a long time. (Dean, 1957: 28–9)

Obviously we want high standards of achievement from handicapped children like all children, but there has to be a place for recognizing what effort has gone into the work. Unreadable it may have been but its message ought to have been loud and clear.

In those days Vera Dean had a very basic form of physiotherapy. Modern physiotherapy is a regular part of the treatment of children with cerebral palsy and there are whole systems of combining physiotherapy with developmental or educative aspects. In those days, the approach was somewhat more pragmatic. Yet the experience of being pulled, pushed, pummelled and twisted even in the most skilful hands causes a measure of discomfort.

We did have some treatment. Some of us were taken to another ward three times a week for drill . . . The young masseuses would walk us up and down and give us simple exercises. They would take our boots off and put their hands under our feet and push. This hurt us very much but if anyone cried with pain they were spoken to sharply by another masseuse. I will never forget the look on some of the children's faces when they had their feet stretched. (ibid.: 30)

A long stay in hospital for a young child can have unfortunate side-effects, cutting him off from many of the everyday experiences of other children, forcing his attention upon the hospital itself as the source of experiences, even his play centres on hospital life. Vera Dean, coming to hospital at twelve, already had a rich store of experiences which others in her ward who had been there longer had never acquired.

Because of my bad speech and because I had lived at home until I was twelve, the other children did not understand me and when they did they did not always believe me because I talked of things they did not know. I was called the 'know-all' and except for talking with little Laurie I grew very quiet and often played by myself. (ibid.: 31)

Her story is of historical interest for in it she tells of the pioneer work in the treatment of cerebral palsy, but its main value is in the direct expression of a childhood physically restrained but with an inner spirit uncrippled. (For a contemporary view of teaching in a hospital ward, see Ann Hales' *The Children of Skylark Ward*.)

Louis Battye's *I Had a Little Nut Tree* is sub-titled 'a reconstruction of childhood' and is one of the outstanding books of its kind. Severely handicapped by cerebral palsy, Mr Battye spent a good deal of his childhood in hospital. After his discharge he was sent home wearing leg-irons and with some help he could stumble around, but not for very long or very far. His hands were 'obstinately' pronated, the fingers stiff, dressing and undressing were difficult and each movement took considerable effort.

Every effort was made to get me to do things for myself. 'Try, try,' I was urged. 'Make your hands work,' and I tried and tried, not always without success. I learned to feed myself

> though not always strictly according to the rules of table etiquette – I could never use a knife effectively – I even learned to pick up a cup to drink without spilling its contents – I was never able to wash myself or comb my hair but did learn to brush my teeth. (Battye, 1966: 34)

These hard won skills sometimes deserted him, especially if he was watched, but given time and an absence of pressure 'I could do easily what half an hour previously had seemed utterly impossible.'

Twice a year the young Battye went back to hospital for a check on his progress. He describes the routine of the consultant with his queue of waiting children and their parents. Children would be undressed ready for the inspection with the consultant surrounded by young medics. And the only way to cope was to switch off mentally while, 'My limbs would be seized, twisted this way and that, flexed and extended, my body poked and kneaded. There would be a rumble of incomprehensible technicalities' (ibid.: 39).

Space does not permit a description of the amateur physiotherapy (provided by a local millhand) his family arranged for him at home, though it is a comic gem. Battye also has many interesting things to say on the additional minor complications of his condition – sensitivity to certain kinds of food, vulnerability to infections, and certain psychological features such as heightened responsiveness to sound, fear of dogs, and what he calls his Freudian reaction to factory chimneys! But most of all we get the strong impression of the sustaining quality of family life which provided a foundation for his developing emotional maturity.

But I want to conclude these extracts from his book by quoting a passage in which he describes his attitude as a child to his handicap.

> Naturally I wished I could walk, but it didn't make me particularly unhappy. When well-meaning adults shook their heads and sighed over me and said, 'It's a thousand pities. I wish you could run about like other little boys', I agreed with them as a matter of course, but privately I thought they were making rather a lot of fuss. I had already developed a species of precocious philosophy to account for the puzzling fact that I couldn't walk and everyone else could. The way I looked at it

was that being able to run about wasn't all fun. Boys who could, like John Berry, frequently fell and hurt themselves: they were naughty and received good hidings from their parents and worst of all they had to go to school to be shut in dreary classrooms and forced to do impossibly hard sums, getting the cane if they did them wrong. I was spared all that. In the long run things even themselves out. There was no essential injustice in life. And sooner or later, probably sooner, I *would* walk. (ibid.: 49–50)

Like disabled adults, handicapped children have to endure the 'Does he take sugar?' syndrome, and young Louis had to wait while his mother recounted his medical history to a sympathetic stranger.

When they addressed me they usually shouted as if I were deaf or an imbecile. I tried to be polite to them as I had been taught, but sometimes it was an effort. (ibid.: 50)

A handicapped childhood need not be a traumatizing experience especially if the child is surrounded by an affectionate and realistic family. The young disabled child frequently evokes feelings of compassion even if the expression of those feelings is clumsy. The young and their families are often sustained by expectations of improvements if not cures. The children themselves are protected from the full realization of their true condition, prognosis and probable niche in society, but at adolescence the 'precocious philosophy' may be put to a severe test. There will be the conventional problems associated with hormonal changes and for some comes the additional complication of a realization of what the future holds for them, as men and women, as employees and as citizens. I think the 'crisis' of adolescence is a specially critical period for disabled young people and how they deal with it and are helped to deal with it, may have much to do with their subsequent adjustment. Recent research (Dalton, 1978) has shown that many handicapped youngsters reach puberty somewhat earlier than their normal peers. Modern attitudes to sex and sexuality in relation to handicap suggests both a greater understanding of needs and their legitimation, though there is some evidence that handicapped teenagers have more limited knowledge of sex than normal peers. Adolescence is sometimes described as a marginal state, and the young person is on the borderline between childhood and adulthood. It is the period during which the transition is marked by a more vigorous demand for independence and experiments in sexual roles. Both these may provide special difficulties for the more severely restricted youngsters. Both are part of the search for a new identity.

Graeme Edwards (*Keep in Touch*, 1962) had infantile glaucoma which left him with little more useful vision than the ability to discriminate between light and dark, yet he succeeded in his chosen career as a reporter (a fascinating account in its own right). Here he describes some of the issues surrounding growing up with a handicap. Although lucky to be part of a large and lively family, his visual handicap seemed to project him onto a different track from his sighted brothers and their friends.

> Life for a blind child, especially with over-timid parents, must often be tremendously lonely – lonely in the sense of being without proper company. I escaped that because I was fifth in a family of five boys, and our house was always full of visitors. Yet, on looking back, I feel sure that some of my tastes and interests and even my relationships with others in the family were deeply influenced by the other form of loneliness blindness can produce, which came from the feeling of isolation, or apartness from the group I was born into. I was never able to have the run of our suburb as my brothers had. I could not go visiting boyhood friends without company. I had no hope of ever riding a bicycle around the neighbourhood like the other kids. And, worst of all, I could not take part in their most exciting activities. So long as I was with only one or two other boys I could frequently join in with what they were doing. But as the group got bigger and the games became too fast-moving or far-flung for me, they always had to make allowances for me and that is a lot to ask of small boys. I was desperately anxious to play cricket, but joining in their matches would have been too dangerous and my parents would have forbidden it.

Finding sport an unsuitable pastime he turned to radio.

In this century the development of radio has brought the world in front of blind people in a way that nothing in the past could have. It is the means of endless entertainment and information without any need to call on someone else to explain, to read aloud, or to translate the material into Braille. Like blindness itself, broadcasting tended to have the effect of driving me into my own company perhaps too much, and separating me from the lives of the rest of the household.

Not only did his special interests separate him from his brothers, he was also to experience special schooling.

As well as my individual approach to amusements and interests imposed by blindness, the other big factor separating me from my family was my need for different schooling. I had been at the Royal Victorian Institute for the Blind for nearly three years when my father was transferred from Western Australia to the head office in Melbourne and all the family went to settle there. In the meantime I boarded at the Institute during the week and stayed at weekends with my father's sister. My brothers, all attending the same private school, were mixing with boys who had much the same backgrounds. Therefore, to a certain degree, conformity was the controller of their views and behaviour. A blind school, on the other hand, like an airforce squadron in wartime, brings together people with widely different upbringings from all social environments. Blindness, when it strikes, does not discriminate between rich and poor, honest and dishonest.

And we read in this excerpt that the school for the blind is not necessarily an over-protected environment.

As I approached the school-leaving age, I had plenty of interests, but compared with those of other teenagers, they were limited and perhaps more intensive. I had always enjoyed going for walks and had sampled competitive sport at the blind school, but I was still not developing many activities out of doors, or regularly mixing with friends of my own age. Most of the people I came into contact with at home were friends of my brothers and, consequently, some years older. . . .

I was constantly on the lookout for indoor games which could be adapted for the use of blind people. When I was eleven I Brailled my first pack of playing cards and had hundreds of hands of German whist, donkey, and later solo and bridge. My top favourite for months was a set of dominoes made with raised dots. Then I went through a craze for draughts, played on a wooden board with indented squares, only to pass both games by after a brother taught me the basic moves in chess. . . .

The years at the blind school in Melbourne were certainly not 'the happiest days of my life', but there at least I was in an atmosphere where I did not need special treatment and it was useless to look for it. Flung together with dozens of other blind children, I was with kids who were physically on a more or less even footing. The amount of sight ranged from zero to strong enough to read big print in newspapers, but most of us could not put our sight to practical use. There was no sympathy or excuse for those who failed in their schoolwork or in playtime activities. We made up our own games, which were quite rough. Everyone was out to win without being held back by any of the reservations which sighted people, playing with us, were inclined to have. (Edwards, 1962: 12–18)

In Marjorie Wallace and Michael Robson's *On Giant's Shoulders* (1976) the story of Terry reached millions through the television programme starring Judi Dench and Bryan Pringle. Terry, although severely handicapped by thalidomide, emerges as a robust, lively and vividly human person. In this excerpt Terry is entering his school.

Despite the large, tougher classes of the comprehensive school, he could still hold his own. He would ride to school in Supercar or drive it up into the back of his father's van and once at school, apart from the toilet, he needed little extra help. The nurse assigned by the local authority to attend to Terry often found herself with little to do.

Terry recalls his first day at his new school, frighteningly large and important. As he drove, Len walking by his side through corridors and classrooms filled with the murmurs of children at work, they came to a carpeted area and Terry was suddenly aware of somebody looking down at him.

'Terry, this is Mr Slater, your new teacher,' said Len.

'Hello, Sir,' Terry said shyly, too overcome to lift himself in his chair.

'Come on up,' said Len.

Terry touched Supercar's controls and in a moment was on a level with his teacher.

'How did you do that?' Mr Slater asked.

Terry explained that he worked the lift with his shoulder, and the apprehension was gone. As he was shown the school, a bell for break rang and the silent corridors were filled with bustling children looking curiously at the little figure in his extraordinary car. Before long Leonard and Mr Slater left him in the library answering questions from a crowd of children.

'Were you born like that, mate?'

'Yes.'

'You haven't got any arms?'

'No, but it doesn't bother me.'

'Witty, ain't you? How old are you?'

'Twelve.'

'What's your name?' asked a small boy.

'Terry.'

'Come on then, Terry. Let's go for a walk.'

'Anything to get away from this mob.'

Terry started Supercar forcing his way through the crowd with his new friend Tony by his side.

That was eighteen months ago. The headmaster, who had been reluctant to take Terry into the school, now admits he has proved himself and is accepted by the other pupils. He has even learned to turn his disabilities to his own advantage. In his machine Terry is more than a match for the toughest bully. His quick wit and well-aimed dummy charges from Supercar soon scatter opponents and have made him a popular ringleader of the classroom gang.

In most school subjects he is average but he is ex-traordinarily well-read – his bookcase is lined with glossy encyclopaedias – and his ability to express himself is far advanced for his age. He has learned to type, using a Posum typewriter adapted by his father with a keyboard of eight micro-switches, but he still prefers to write with his rudimentary feet. (Wallace and Robson, 1976: 164)

We are fortunate in having had one writer who was not only able to portray the childhood world of a handicapped child, but to do so in a transcendent way. Christy Brown's *My Left Foot* (1972) marked the emergence of a gifted artist, and choosing an excerpt from his book is tantalizing for it is full of good writing, insights and wisdom.

In the early part of the book he describes his lively and loving family and his beginnings as an artist and a writer. The following extract is from that period of his life where he is poised between childhood and the adult world. By thirteen he had made considerable progress, he was using his paintings as a means of expressing and giving shape to his feelings and this immersion in painting came at a time when he was sensing a measure of change in family relationships. He was in love with Jenny with her brown curls, lively green eyes and pouting lips, and as he says 'my heart was still miles ahead of my body in growth and development'. Christy and Jenny exchange notes, she is shown his paintings, and he is convinced he has a friend in the best-looking girl in the street.

> That evening before she left, Jenny sat very quietly, toying idly with the book, a little frown creasing her forehead and her lower lips pushed out, as she always looked when she wanted to say something difficult. After a little while she got up, then suddenly knelt down on the grass beside me and kissed me very tenderly on the forehead. I drew back, surprised, bewildered, for she had never kissed me before. (Brown, 1972: 63)

Jenny runs out of the garden and from his dream. He paints wildly 'haphazard slices of boiling mind dashed on to the paper wildly and recklessly'. Then one day he catches Jenny looking at him:

> It was a look of pity. I knew then, as I came to know many times later, how bitter and crushing a simple look of pity can be to someone like myself who needs something other than sympathy – the strength that only genuine human affection can give to the weakened heart.
>
> For a few blissful weeks I had allowed myself to dream that I was a normal, ordinary boy of fourteen, who thought himself in love . . . and vain enough to think that she cared for him in return. Now all that make-believe was at an end, but the

bitterest of all was the realization that I had tricked myself into believing that my affliction did not matter, that my 'queerness' was more self-consciousness which nobody else took any notice of. I can see what an ass I had been to fool myself so magnificently. (ibid.: 65)

Occasionally the combination of parenting a handicapped child and exceptional literary gifts come together to make a work of considerable literary merit. Many of the accounts by parents make for interesting reading but only exceptionally do they rise to the level of literature. One such example and my personal favourite in the genre is Paul West's *Words for a Deaf Daughter*, a daunting title for such a splendidly written work. It opens with a memorably atmospheric account of his daughter's room, festooned with paintings, collages, models and items collected on walks. Here he introduces us to his daughter and the childhood world of deafness through her school report.

Your lip-reading rubric has this beneath it: *Understands familiar words through lip-reading and hearing. Span of attention for assimilating new vocabulary is still short.*

Yes, and I know you can be incorrigibly frivolous about new words, few of which you ever seem to think you need, but I have also seen you checking through your physiognomy at a mirror, saying the words loudly and almost correctly while the bits of the head they denote remain in place. As they say in the report under Speech Aptitude: you imitate *many sounds very well, with an accurate reproduction of intonation too*: but they go on to note how you are easily distracted from concentrated speech work (so was I, if it's any comfort to you, until about twenty-five). Always, you have taken or left speech as you thought fit, and no bribe or coercion will work, but only a counter-distraction equivalent to gold over silver, radioactivity over magnetism, Samarkand over Acapulco . . . The house is crammed with attention-getters, just to get you to *look* – and as soon as you looked, they took the baubles away in order to work with the attention you gave while it lasted. Which often wasn't long: time for a word, a plosive, a round O, concessions you perfunctorily made to a word-obsessed rest of the world. (West, 1970: 11)

His daughter was commended for her motor skills and liking for
pattern.

Of pattern, all I'll say is that your passion for design and
symmetry would have done credit to a mediaeval theologian.
Somewhere in your head you kept a kind of DNA pattern of the
attitudes and millimetrical relationships in which you wanted
things to be – slippers, cutlery, cushions, curtains, rugs and
pokers, all such. I have seen you develop an apostate rage
because, somewhere in the house, there was a bottle with an
imperfectly placed top, or because someone was ingorging
with the wrong spoon. If there is to be an argument for design
then at some point you must surely have been dispatched to
earth as a special proof. (ibid.: 12)

Energetic: says the report.

Which is like calling the cheetah not backwards in moving
forward or the elephant heavier than air . . . a compulsive,
rapid and exquisitely co-ordinated mover. You have over-run
us all while working out of your system something that you
inhale back again with each breath; and so, on it goes, this
unquenchable agitation of your legs and arms, that never quite
matches the rhythm of your high-pitched, looping call. (ibid.:
13)

While she has been noted for playing happily alongside other
children she does not enter into their play:

Simply, you never had any practice and had not realized that
suddenly you were permitted to play with other children. I
have never seen you refuse to play with any consenting adult
in private or in public, but of course, then you played
exceedingly rough. (ibid.: 14)

The final comment in the report suggests that she is difficult to
assess.

Brain Damage (?)
The question mark sums up a good deal of the considerable
amount said about you over the past years and either cancelled
or left dubiously standing. It is clear that, more often than
occasionally, something in your head doesn't work as it ought
to: something that seems to be tied up with your hearing
poorness. What? I wish I knew. The words that crop up, brain

damage, middle brain damage, nerve deafness, autism, dyslexia, etc. give us no more than an illusion of command, or of
knowing, yet I have known parents, who, wanting
passionately to have their child diagnosed, refuse the specific
label when it comes . . . Whatever might be the total of the
explanation of the things wrong with you, let me tell you – in
case, maybe, you've been too busy to realize it – exuberant
play, and emphatic response has worked minor wonders with
you already – so has school. (ibid.: 15)

The child's passion for order he suggests comes from an
insecurity as to whether the world will be there the next day
('precariousness in a world of silence'). But she has learned and
has things to learn. She does not know her surname, towns,
addresses, does know where the *wun tu three* counting chart
belongs, what coat goes on which hook – slow to speak, slow to
walk, making up for it by running everywhere – loves water,
umbrellas, has an invisible friend, three words, and in her head
the 'tinnitus of bad bells'.

He contrasts the limited perceptions that clinicians can have of
children only seen in a formal test situation.

You haven't seen her do the living things: give creation a run
for its money . . . They haven't seen you like a gross Ophelia
distribute round the house – on the window ledges, in the
wardrobe between two decent suits or dresses, on the rim of
the letter box, on the Christmas tree itself – pork sausages in
butchers' hooks or threaded on wire coat hangers. Or eat
sausages raw, oblivious of worms. Or, in hydrodynamic
delight, rip off shoes and socks to plant your bare feet on the
TV screen whenever it showed water. Or . . . sit naked and
warbling for an hour in a wash basin of cold water, or green
your face, eat nail varnish, coat the windows with lavender
furniture polish, jump down five stairs fearlessly, mimic . . .
men carrying umbrellas, chant into a toilet pedestal after
choking it with a whole roll of tissue, chew cigarettes, cover
yourself with Bandaids when there wasn't a scratch in sight,
climb my ladder and refuse to descend, slide pencils up your
nose . . . eat six bananas in six minutes . . . cut your hair at
random . . . rock so hard your head touched the floor . . . sit
motionless and rapt in front of a mirror. (ibid.: 25)

During one of the examinations his daughter is given an audiometric test, with pure tones of different pitches and volume.

> Then with audio equipment the technician makes contact . . . your expression changes, fixing in atavistic wonder. Funny, it was as if we were watching the face of sound itself while you, flushed and nervous heard something invisible . . . confronting for the first time your share of the missing continent. I felt a bit like shouting myself. I'd never heard anyone hearing before. (ibid.: 26)

With the help of hearing aids, induction loops and expert tuition the little girl began to make progress towards the hearing world. She is now

> a girl who can make beds (sometimes six sheets to a bed), bake black bread, fry bacon tin hard, iron and fold clothes with the finesse of a weight-lifter, hoover the carpet, mow the lawn, more or less lay the table, adjust the TV, fell apples from the tree by swotting it with a tennis racquet, tune your own hearing aids, and on your best days butter bread and most days recite your first name . . . at the school for the deaf, a day girl, almost six. You have become unoffendably gregarious, have learned to hold hands . . . you have discovered how NO doubles the range of your concepts . . . long and agile, you have a vocabulary, a school bag and homework book. (ibid.: 30)

Finally we come to some extracts from Dorcas Munday's *Opportunity Not Pity* (1976). Miss Munday has to spend much of her life in a wheelchair and her story was written with a pencil in between her teeth 'pecking at the typewriter is much the same fashion as an industrious hen in a barnyard'. 'Dorcas', she discovered, means gazelle, but 'to all intents and normal everyday purposes – I was, from birth, helpless'.

> It is very difficult for me to remember early childhood and I cannot recall any given moment when I realized that I was most severely handicapped and therefore different from other children. I do remember sitting up in a specially-made high-chair and lying down in a large Victorian-type pram. I cried a lot and poor Mother was never sure whether this was pain or bad temper – I suspect it was a bit of both! . . .

My extreme disability necessitated a very sheltered life and my father carried me everywhere. Relatives visited and my cousins, who were about my age, would run and skip like most children and I cannot remember that I had any great desire to do the same. Even when I left school at sixteen I had not come to realize quite what was going on – there was no yardstick by which I could assess my disabilities and others' abilities. Schools for 'The Handicapped' are partly to blame here. If, during all your formative years, you are in the company of others who are equally disabled and the only folk who are normally equipped are those who look after you, you cannot estimate your own physical failings and neither can you truly come to practical terms with them. . . .

At the age of eight I was sent, as a weekly boarder, to the John Greenwood Shipman School in Northampton. My six months there were not the happiest of my life. We were taught to read but in so many respects it was more like hospital than school, although I believe that conditions there in that respect are now much improved. With too many people around to act as 'mother' to the young, their maturity is delayed. And of course, like so many kiddies who are sent to boarding school, I was homesick. The school was not over-protective, we were encouraged to ride about on specially-constructed bicycles and to walk up and down between parallel bars and then, at eight-and-a-half, I was transferred to St Margaret's at Croydon as a full-time boarder. Again boarding did not suit me. Miss Evans was the most outstanding personality of this phase in my young life. She was not only a great teacher; she was a remarkably understanding and patient woman who helped and encouraged me tremendously. I should have been happy there – but others were as handicapped as I. I did make friends but never mixed with able-bodied youngsters and we played a lot with dolls – well, when you're that handicapped your play activities are limited.

As to artificial equipment, I was then wearing spectacles to correct a squint and callipers on my legs to help me walk. I was never keen on those callipers. The housemothers were adept at lifting them on and kept our other physical problems to a minimum. In those days, not so far distant, callipers were the accepted equipment for handicapped folk. They kept my legs steady and although I could not walk in them they did give me some small measure of independence. . . .

I fed myself at school but I don't nowadays – the involuntary movements of my arms and hands delay the process of getting through a meal and of course the food gets cold and I don't, in the presence of other people, like my handicap to be made more obvious by those same sudden movements. Throwing one's food around, no matter that it's not intentional, does not endear one to one's neighbours or create quite the right impression for ease of table intercourse. . . .

At twelve, another move, this time to Thomas Delarue School, Tonbridge, Kent. For two years, I remember, I liked it but I became lonely. I was always a bit of a loner anyway, with no very close friends, and those friends I made in my first two years at Tonbridge were older than I and I soon left the school. Not all of us, handicapped or ambulant, are completely community-minded by nature, are we? But this is something which the former must develop. They depend on more mobile people for the most basic services and, if they are to develop communications with the rest of mankind, they have to seek out the herd. A fully mobile person can afford the luxury of being a loner. The handicapped, if they are to receive necessary help and make their lives more interesting than just sitting in their chairs, at the risk of becoming cabbages, must learn to mix. I didn't cry in my loneliness – just went away to a classroom to read a book. This was more rewarding to me than sitting, mindlessly, watching one television programme after another, but in the end it was this sudden spell of loneliness which made me leave. I stayed at Tonbridge until I was sixteen-and-a-half years old. The transition from school to the 'outside world' was a shock – it was as if someone had whipped away rose-tinted spectacles. . . .

Wellingborough was where I came to live with my family. A strange place for me in my strange situation. I was confronted by loneliness again – loneliness of a different kind. The experience was a little like being born again into another world – a world which until then I didn't know existed.

Dorcas Munday writes that, in her experience, visible disabilities spark off some chain of reaction in normal people with an almost inevitable link between physical abnormality and mental subnormality. She noted that this capacity is in people of all ages.

It's not only the young and unthinking. People who, you presume, will have matured, can prove as ignorant when brought into the presence of a severely disabled person. Two able-bodied friends of mine were pushing my chair up a steep hill at Ryde when we encountered a small boy with his mother. With engaging and quite innocent frankness the little boy said, 'Isn't she a big baby!' We all smiled but mother didn't – 'Come on!' – she just didn't have the poise to carry it off – 'you mustn't say that to the lady.' So vigorous was her rebuke, so urgent her order, the little boy ran off quickly, fell and began to cry. Mother had 'spoiled what might have been a beautiful friendship' – or at least an exchange of pleasantries with the child who knew no better – instead he was actually scared of me through his mother's embarrassment and desire to get away. . . .

People who have matured considerably in all other respects sometimes appear to have missed out somewhere along the way of their many years of life and one finds it harder to dismiss their thoughtlessness – far harder than the dismissal of a child's artless observation, if one is to judge from the remarks of a coach-load of senior citizens parked near our coach at the end of a happy outing. In those sickly rising and falling tones which so many older folk adopt when addressing very young children – or perhaps lap dogs! – We were treated to 'Ah! Look!' – 'Have you enjoyed yourselves, my dears?' and then, to each other, and as if we were a set of rather attractive monkeys in a zoo cage, 'I wonder if they would like some sweets?' We warm to understanding and kindness but freeze up under such silly patronage. It's well-meant but so ill-considered. Two other senior citizens at Whipsnade Zoo were not so benevolent when I was with my friend, Margaret Spearman, her brother David, and Jim, his friend, who were pushing our chairs. We reached a clearing where the lads put on our brakes and, as young folk will, without any apparent preamble, started fooling around promoting a giggling fit in all of us. The two old dears didn't approve and, tut-tutting, one said, 'Really, they shouldn't let them out!' This illustrates the need in a non-ambulant person's character for an inexhaustible sense of the ridiculous – in short, if you don't learn to discover the funny side in such situations you will spend your life in tears. . . .

Wheelchairs mean different things to different people – in Rome, Margaret did quite well when several people gave her small coins, thinking she was a beggar! At a bazaar in Collingtree I was literally the captive audience of a well-meaning Job's comforter who obviously associated my wheelchair with truly chronic suffering and the exchange went:
'How are you?'
'I'm fine, thank you very much', and I was – feeling fine and thoroughly enjoying myself.
'Yes,' darkly, 'You look alright, but I don't expect you feel at all well – do you?'

This, as they say, 'put the mockers' on a nice outing and I was reminded of the chap who visited his old friend ill in bed at home and observed, 'Awkward stairs to get a coffin down – ain't they?' You see, we don't want that sort of commiseration either. The lady obviously though that I was permanently ill. In fact I am a healthy girl – organically fit in body and, I hasten to add, in mind also. . . .

There are some experiences one has in a wheelchair which require all one's understanding but in the end one must put it down to plain, mindless bad manners and not funny in the twisted way that being taken as mentally defective may be rendered funny (one experience of which earned me the alliterative nickname 'Mental Munday!'). I was once taken to a 'normal' youth club – one for the able-bodied – and wheeled into the cloakroom to leave my coat but my helper was called away and, left alone, I had to find someone to help me get my coat off. Two girls were there. I tried to speak to them to tell them that they could help me with my coat. They turned to each other and giggled. It hurt dreadfully but it does no good to try to reason with such people – they don't even know they are being spiteful. . . .

Honesty is the best tonic for us and we can spot it in an instant even if folk, unaccustomed to meeting the severely disabled, are only trying; we have learned enough tolerance ourselves to overlook their concealed discomfort and to allow the preliminaries to ease the atmosphere gradually until the person loses shyness and gradually becomes more at ease – they are trying. Honesty, true honesty, however, is the gift of the very young, as in the twelve-year-old Girl Guide whom I met at an international camp and whom I asked what she'd expected to see when she'd learned that I was coming. The answer was short, honest and, to me at that moment, refreshingly funny – 'A monster with no arms or legs,' she replied truthfully. In a subsequent, sober moment, however, I did reflect on this. If an intelligent near-teenager thought that – what preconceived ideas would the rest of the world and his wife have before meeting Dorcas? . . .

Perhaps I shall be able to dispel the notion that because we are almost entirely dependent upon others for help with such fundamental exercises as feeding ourselves, due to the in-voluntary jerks of our limbs caused by our disability, and moving from place to place in our chairs, we can, nevertheless, think and feel for ourselves and that, as a friend of mine expressed it pithily, while we may have to stay sitting down while we are thinking, we are not sitting on our brains! (Munday, 1976: 7–14)

It is through such accounts we may come to a richer understand-ing of a handicapped childhood and how that experience comes to shape the growing person.

Peter Coveney's (1967) *The Image of Childhood* has the sub-title 'The individual and society' which reminds us that each recollec-tion of childhood takes place not only in a specific familial context, but in a social context of time, place and attitudes. So each contribution to the literature of childhood impaired by sensory or physical damage is, in a sense, an historical document, not merely autobiography but an image of a time. If they are to be used as anything more than historically interesting anecdotes they have to address themselves to more enduring themes, or rather we may read them in search of such themes. One theme is negative in instinct for by reading accounts of an individual childhood we may avoid the arid generalizations of the psychological child, the psychiatric child and the sociological child. The other is positive, for through these accounts, when they are touched with honesty and self-knowledge, we may come to 'taste life' as Rousseau has it and our task is to do what we can to ensure that the 'bird born for joy' can still 'sit in a cage and sing'.

Summary

The relative scarcity of childhood accounts provided by disabled people make them correspondingly more valuable. It is difficult enough for an adult to cross over into the world of childhood and to see the world as it is perceived by the young and possibly harder to imagine a childhood without sight or movement or sound. As with all children, handicapped children's primary social system, their family, provides the location in which they learn who they are and how they are valued. As with other aspects of handicap there is no typical childhood experience, for each child will experience a unique set of relationships and from these the themes of relationships with parents and brothers and sisters, treatment, schooling and adolescence were selected as being of major significance. In this period the child's attitude to his handicap will be shaped and the accounts we have illustrate that children develop a personal philosophy which enables them to cope. Special schooling alongside others equally or more seriously handicapped appears to be a mixed fortune, for some leading to realization of differences, while for others forging bonds with others similarly affected. The mainstreaming of handicapped children in regular schools is always the preferred option when this is compatible with needs. Figuring large in the accounts referred to is the experience of separation, treatment and hospitalization where so often things are mediated to children rather than explained. Through such accounts we can re-examine our attitudes and relationships with handicapped children.

10
The normality of handicap

The making of handicap

If impairment can be described objectively, handicap is a perception, a social judgement, a value judgement. In part, such perceptions arise from general social values – from the kinds of persons we are – and also from specific experiences. Whether it is social values (such as the premium placed on physique and appearance), our degree of authoritarianism, or the amount of knowledge or information we may have of disablement which contribute most to the formation of this perception is open to debate. What is accepted as beyond dispute is that disabled people constitute a handicapped segment of society. Their disadvantages are of many kinds – financial, educational, in housing and mobility, vocational and inter-personal; and I would add one more – professionalization.

In arguing that society 'manufactures' handicap we must take care not to overstate the case and imply that the problems of disabled people are other people, or that the limitations due to impairments are not real. I wish to contend that among the problems confronting disabled people is the perception of both lay and professional people. Such perceptions may be subject to significant change and transformation or, more dangerously, be re-coded and re-emerge as new labels or slogans which give rise to the illusion of progress while leaving the basic structure of perception and behaviour unchanged, so that the rhetoric of acceptance and normalization may not be translated into a social reality.

While noting the encouraging progress that has been made on several fronts (preventative medicine, pre- and post-natal services, screening of school children, special schooling, family finance, the provision of aids, etc., it seems to me that there is yet another side to the story. Too many disabled people are institutionalized; are subject to downright discrimination in the job market; have to fight bureaucratic systems for basic entitlements; have an inadequate communication-system through which new techniques and aids are made known and available to them; are under-represented in positions of influence in the institutions and agencies which are there to serve them; are seldom placed in positions of public eminence to serve as a focus for attitude change; are infrequently portrayed by the media in a naturalistic way; and seem to lack effective political power at all levels from local to national. It is this combination which creates handicap.

Among the most potent sources of social identity given to a disabled person is his or her impairment. Visible impairments have a way of affecting our perceptions of the person in such a manner that the impairment becomes a significant stimulus in provoking a social judgement. When we know that 'x' is blind or that 'y' is a paraplegic, we seem to have to hand the most vital piece of information which is necessary for forming a view of that person. In impression-formation such basic building-blocks enable us to construct a complex series of behavioural expectations from which we can interpret all the 'information' the person gives us about himself. Visible impairments have become crucial indicators not only of the presence of functional limitations but produce secondary generalizations which shape interactional processes and gives embodiment to social value-judgements. One way of expressing this is to say that 'handicap' becomes integral with 'personality'; knowing that someone is blind or deaf is to 'know' their most important piece of biographical evidence – although this is not true. The 'knowledge' also allows us to explain the person – he is a high achiever *because* he is blind, or bitter and inadequate *because* he's in a wheelchair. Perceptions of handicap become an important element in a primitive theory of personality and behaviour.

This primitive perceptual process derives its potency from dominant social values which seem to find it easy to imply a relationship between a physical impairment and emotional, behavioural and attitudinal factors – that is, impairment seems to imply handicap. Deviation from the norm in physique and appearance, and its correlative behavioural consequences, are of course not simply statistical, neutral deviations, they possess negative value loadings, and since they are negatively valued the possessor of such differences must surely share our perception and apply that perception and those values to himself. By a process of spreading, the localized infection of difference becomes the epidemic of deviance. It is the experience of many disabled men and women to have had a history of learned inferiority. This history results in styles of behaviour among disabled people who have been overwhelmed by the indoctrination process which reinforces popular persuasion and social oppression and is rationalized by appeals to biology. (He is like that because he is blind, deaf, in a wheelchair, etc.) Individuals who transcend popular stereotypes have to be explained by exceptional motivation or talents which leave the stereotype and the social structures unmodified.

So effective has the process of social typing been that sociologists have been able to identify distinctive roles which are allocated to disabled people (e.g. helped person, public relations man for his category of disability). Either there is something so special about disability that disabled people take up special roles within society, or society perceives disability as a distinctive state and casts persons into these distinctive roles, and the latter seems the only tenable view. As long as it is possible to describe the life of disabled people as consisting of a set of specialized roles which on the whole are negatively valued, then society has failed in its normative objective or succeeded in its objective of stigmatization although the oppressive relationship is now more clearly understood.

At the very core of compassion and care for disabled people is still the concept that they are a group who need to have things done for and to them (which is true) but only fairly recently has it become possible for the helping agencies to conceive of disabled people as possessing a viewpoint of their own, as having the capacity to make informed judgements about the nature and quality of services *they* feel they need, and even more recently has emerged the beginnings of a more strident demand among the disabled to plead their own case and fight their own battles.

In summary then I am persuaded that one of the failures of our society is not in its treatment of disabled people (though there are wide gaps and inequalities here) nor in its lack of sensitivity to needs (as long as the asymmetry of power and prestige is maintained) but in its failure to comprehend the normality of handicap. It is the overwhelming insistence that we perceive and encourage 'the disabled' to perceive themselves as deviant that is the root of the problem. Impairment makes a difference, but society seems to insist that it is a mark of deviance-nature and accidents may create disability; we manufacture handicap.

Prevention

The second way in which we make handicap is our national reluctance to take seriously the notion of prevention. Margaret and Arthur Wynn in their *Prevention of Handicap and the Health of Women* (1979) note that in Britain there is an annual flow of 30,000 children impaired from birth. In the struggle to reduce this incidence a combined approach is needed, involving not only medical and health care professionals but a whole new philosophy of social care which, because of its importance and cost, requires a major public commitment to the concept of preventing impairment. Comparative evidence from Scandinavia shows that the determined application of policies can reduce the incidence of some major causes of impairment. Alongside the capacity to reduce incidence is the fact that modern techniques make the survival of damaged infants more likely; of those who survive, the life expectation is greatly increased, and so the proportion of those who survive and who are severely handicapped has also grown. Wynn and Wynn (p. 11) show how, in Sweden, the incidence of cerebral palsy has fallen from 2.2 cases per 1000 (1954) to 1.3 cases per 1000 (1970), a 40 per cent fall in sixteen years. The incidence of cerebral palsy in Britain is estimated as about twice the Swedish figure. Prevention in Scandinavia has focused on improved ante-perinatal care and there are no minority or disadvantaged groups who miss out on the excellent quality of care for pregnant mothers. In contrast, little advance has been made with respect to Down's Syndrome in terms of prevention but amniocentesis makes the detection of a chromosomally affected foetus possible. In Britain the birthrate of Down's Syndrome babies to women over 40 years of age accounts for about 100 cases out of 1000 yet amniocentesis is confined to women over the age of 40. Wynn and Wynn suggest that effective application of amniocentesis would reduce the incidence of Down's Syndrome by 10 per cent. In America one estimate is that the *application of current knowledge* would reduce the present incidence of developmental disabilities by about 50 per cent. In Britain the Spastics Society campaign 'Save a Baby' proclaimed that 40 per cent of cases of cerebral palsy could be prevented not by new technology but by the thorough use of proven methods. Wynn and Wynn describe the prevention of handicap as in 'the spirit of our age' but they argue that such preventative measures as are necessary cannot be left to just the engaged professional, and demand a societal response which applauds the selection of prevention as a priority in the national scheme of things. The signs of such a priority moving from rhetoric to resources are few.

Similar claims have been made (Stein, 1975; Conley, 1974) about the possibility of reducing the incidence of mild mental retardation through planned programmes of raising the quality of the general environment of the urban poor, and specific family- and community-based programmes of language and learning skills. The cost-effectiveness of intervention to reduce the incidence of mild mental retardation could be calculated against the lowered costs of special services and the promise of greater earning capacities and greater self-help and its correlative lessening of need for a range of social services. Conley suggests that effective intervention in this field ought to be a priority 'if the entire [American] population had the same prevalence of persons with IQs below 50 as middle- and upper-class whites, the number of persons in this range would decline by about 55 per cent' (Conley, 1974: 24). From a number of sources it seems the know-how exists to make significant inroads into the incidence of handicap, and the failure to make effective use of that knowledge speaks volumes for indifference and neglect. We are content to allow the manufacture of handicap to continue unchecked.

Barriers

Frank Bowe (1978) in his *Handicapping America* identifies six major barriers to the integration of disabled people into society: architectural, attitudinal, educational, occupational, legal and personal. On architectural barriers he notes some problems which illustrate these issues: if a citizen of Woodbridge (NJ) wishes to exercise his prerogative under a US Supreme Court decision to present a case to his local seat of government he has to get up twenty-three steps to enter the building and a further twenty-three to gain access to the right office. He also records the number of schools not adapted for pupils with wheelchairs and how Washington, DC's rapid transport system (METRO) which was intended to be designed for handicapped and elderly users as well as able-bodied was still unusable by the disabled twelve years after its commencement because the builders were still haggling over putting in an elevator at one of its stations. He records that getting legislation for a barrier-free environment is easier than translating that legislation into action. From Braille notices, printed notices for the deaf, the siting of elevator buttons, doors wide enough for wheelchairs, suitable lavatories, to ramps of easy gradient, much more needs to be done to make the physical environment open to the handicapped. Our own position is not noticeably better.

Of the attitudinal barriers he comments on covert rejection (since politeness does not permit overt negative reactions) and describes experiments which show how the able-bodied when talking to the handicapped smiled and gave opinions they did not hold for fear of offending handicapped people. Bowe notes the awkwardness and falseness of many encounters between the two and concludes that this awkwardness reaches out to all levels including that of policy. 'We applaud stories about "super-cripples" yet segregate disabled children in basement classrooms and isolated institutions' (p. 23). National leadership shows the same uncertainty with valuable resources being spent on income supplements and not on training and job placements.

Educational barriers are those which segregate children by virtue of their disabilities and these barriers operate not just at the level of basic schooling but in further and higher education. One worthy body declared that California State University would present no problems to disabled students, but David Travis, an Assistant Dean at CSUC, found only one campus out of fourteen meeting the needs of disabled students. In this country a survey by the National Union of Students (1976) found that though more disabled students were entering further and higher education, only 34 per cent of pupils from special schools capable of entering further and higher education were able to do so. The survey showed a significant number of colleges and university premises were simply not adapted to the needs of disabled people. The recommendations of the NUS report (pp. 28–30) – adaptation of buildings to conform with the requirements of the Chronically Sick and Disabled Persons Act, 1970, applications treated solely on academic merit, each institution to include information for disabled students in prospectuses, the setting up of institutional committees to oversee needs of disabled students and their special financial needs – have made their impact, but progress has been slow and uneven. To the forefront of improving provision and changing attitudes has been the vigorous National Bureau for Handicapped Students.

The barriers to work for the disabled are many and various. Herbert (1977) noted that 'at least one firm in five was failing to comply with legislation requiring them to employ a quota of disabled people.' (An employer with more than twenty employees must fill 3 per cent of his workforce with disabled people.) Prosecutions for failure to comply with the law are few and there is only a small number of inspectors (ten for the whole country in 1977). The official register of disabled people who are unemployed probably underestimates the size of the total problem for there are people who prefer not to 'register' fearing this will harm their job prospects. The whole question of the quota system is in dispute, but there is good evidence that even within government departments quotas were not being filled. (One survey showed only three out of thirty meeting their quota obligations.) Mr Alfred Morris, MP, in a letter of July 1978, noted that while gains had been made in the area of social security benefit, Invalid Car Allowances, Mobility Allowances, the 'Motability' scheme and the Family Fund, grants to employers for the adaptation of work premises and the Job-Introduction Scheme, it was 'particularly difficult to improve the employment opportunities of disabled people at a time when unemployment among people generally remains high. The percentage of the severely disabled workforce that is unemployed is greater than that of the workforce as a whole and, clearly, sheltered employment is not immune from the current difficulties.' An editorial in *Euroforum* (1980) showed that similar problems were affecting disabled people within the European Economic Community and that the European Social Fund had benefited some 72,000 persons with disabilities, increasing the opportunities for training, but commented that 'sadly, even good vocational training is no guarantee of a job'. In a society dominated by the morality of the market-place the disabled would appear to be among the most vulnerable sections of the workforce. Even when employment is offered, it is often a low paid form of work and the match between abilities and occupation is frequently imperfect. As well as unemployment we also have under-employment.

Bowe mentions the legal barriers which disabled people have to surmount. One of the interesting questions here is why it took so long to get legislation such as the 1970 Chronically Sick and Disabled Persons Act onto the statute book or why we had to wait until 1970 for mentally handicapped children to be considered as suitable for 'education' rather than training, and why a report like 'Integrating the Disabled' was published as late as 1974. It seems to me that while there are still legal obstacles in the path of some disabled (the requirement in some job applications to disclose epilepsy, for example), the most important obstacle facing the disabled is the bureaucratic jungle – the tangled web of legislation, rights, allowances and claiming procedures. Indeed, so complex has this matter become that a new professional has emerged – the Welfare Rights Officer. 'Like the high priests of old, to act as an intermediary between the layman and the law – in this case the morass of welfare benefits' (Simkins and Tickner, 1978: 36). The same source also acknowledges the gap between legislative intent and action. Specifically, the Chronically Sick and Disabled Persons Act sets out the duties of local authorities to discover the number of disabled people, to provide a wide range of services (practical assistance in the home, help with recreation, transport, holidays, housing), and deals with the modification of public buildings, representation of disabled people on advisory bodies, allowing invalid carriages on footpaths, the 'orange badge' scheme and many others. It is seen by some as a splendid charter for the disabled and a permanent monument to its principal architect, Alf Morris. Over and above its detailed recommendations there was a new philosophy of hope, dignity and a sense of community responsibility. Concepts like rights, respect and dignity were intoxicating ideas for disabled people whose everyday experience of bureaucracy was of complexity, delay, uncertainty and mistrust. Simkins and Tickner are confident that the Act has created 'bitter disappointment'. This bitterness has grown in an economic climate which has inhibited the expansion of services. The implementation of the Act was further hindered by the reorganization of National Health structures, the discouragement by central government of local attempts to implement parts of the Act, and by varied regional interpretations of the Act giving rise to unfair and unequal treatment in different parts of the country. All of these were compounded by the expansion of means tests, payment scales and criteria for services and allowances which were estimated as being equivalent to 7000 means tests.

> Last but not least, so much attention was paid by press and television to the . . . Act . . . that for every disabled person who found his 'right' to a television set or a telephone to be purely theoretical, there are dozens of able-bodied television watchers now convinced that anyone who is disabled will be pampered from the cradle to the grave, with telly all the way! . . . many people now genuinely believe that all the provisions of the 1970 Act are a reality for all disabled people. There is no understanding that disabled people have never been further from that 'control over their own incomes' which Beveridge saw as essential to the freedom of any citizen, nor the opportunity to use what abilities they have to contribute to the community. Nor is it generally understood that the effect of each new benefit or service announced may not be to add to the income of those who qualify for it, but often merely to change the label on the part of the little they already get, while at the same time adding to the complexity of the choices they must make as to how to obtain the best total deal within their total 'entitlements'. (Simkins and Tickner, 1978: 32)

They conclude that the able-bodied have lost interest in the disabled, assuming all their needs are 'met' under the Act.

Bowe's last barrier he called the personal barrier and he comments that adventitious disability results in problems of daily living, reduced social status, decreased income and 'lowered perceptions of their own worth as human beings'. Life-long disablement is frequently associated with an 'inferior education and preparation for life [being] segregated from normals and sheltered from the harsh realities that await them as adults' (p. 35), and the stress of confronting a harsh world makes this group attribute their misfortunes to their disabilities. In such a context 'passing' as normal becomes an 'over-riding concern'. In other words, to be disabled is to be a shamed person.

To this list of barriers I would add one more: the professionaliz-ation of handicap. Handicap has become the happy-hunting-ground of many professional interests. Handicap is the province of the medical specialist, the educational psychologist, the social worker, the welfare rights worker, the residential care worker, the special teacher, the health visitor and the occupational therapist. Each cadre of professional concern develops its own cognitive style of appraising the handicap, with its in-group jargon, house journals, specialized training and shared value-systems. Not only does this present problems of inter-disciplinary communication which has been endlessly bewailed and lamented, but it lends itself to the process of mystification. Each skill and craft likes to present what it does in a shape and form which gives professional respectability to its work and practitioners. The cumulative effect of this multi-professional mystification has been to create a powerful sense of specialized activity which can only be understood effectively by those properly initiated into the mystery. The elevation of tasks to this level has its correlative in the mystification of the treatment of handicap which further removes the handicap from the realm of normality. Professional mysti-fication enhances the social distance between the normal com-munity and disabled people by reassuring the community that specialized help is available for people who are different; thus the difference is maintained. If we were totally honest we might admit that many of our deeply held theories about 'adjustment to handicap', the 'personality of the disabled person' and 'methods of treatment' are often challenged by common sense and practical experience and that some of the most effective ways of helping disabled people arise out of their contribution not ours – a potential slowly being appreciated.

The making of handicapped women

A question suggests itself. Are disabilities and impairments more handicapping for women than men? An instant retort is that both sexes are affected in the same way – in personal reaction and in their experiences of society's attitudes to disability. Jo Campling in *Better Lives for Disabled Women* (1979) suggests that there is a double handicap of stereotyped expectations for behaviour as a woman and as a disabled person. In some ways the feminine role may be adapted to the disabled role and Campling cites acceptance of dependency and willingness to seek help as examples. She writes that one of the major problems of the disabled woman is coming to terms with her 'spoiled body image' since 'outward appearance is often particularly important to women' and 'the female condition, idealized in many cultures as nurturing, responsive and attractive to men, carries additional pressures for the disabled woman'. In her book Campling discusses marital relationships, sexuality, menstruation, menopause, pregnancy, motherhood, clothing, being at home, education and employment, benefits and sources of advice and in forty odd pages she manages to condense a considerable amount of practical help and insight into the lives of disabled women. Flat, unadorned statements challenge the reader at many points but the central concept is the idea of the collision of two separate roles – that of woman and disabled person – and one image may be taken to stand for that conjunction; one of the disabled women reported to her how as a teenager she was taken out by her boyfriend in her wheelchair and people 'assumed she must be his relative because they could not accept her as a typical girl able to attract a boy friend'.

Campling's *Images of Ourselves* (1981) records a series of conversations with women who are disabled and this volume adds a vivid experiential dimension to the themes raised in her earlier book. Many of these themes, such as society's imposed values on appearance and body shape which have a special significance for women with visible impairments, are similar to the views expressed by Susan Sontag (1972) on the double standards which apply to women in relation to ageing. In Campling's compilation there is a strong sense of the interaction between the radicalization of disability and that set of values, beliefs and attitudes rather inadequately conveyed by the term 'women's movement'. The impression is conveyed that these articulate women came to their comprehension of society's attitudes to disability through the consciousness developed through the struggle for women's rights. Their perspective on disabilities and women is not just to perceive a parallel process in which they were discriminated against and disadvantaged like other minority groups but rather a growing sense of the manifold ways in which expectations for women compounded the 'disabled role'. One of the women describes this process in her own life beginning with a gradual realization of how the 'system' (education, the law, the institution of marriage, medicine and language itself) combined to place women in a socially inferior position. From these insights she went on to discover in herself the ways in which she had been treated as a 'disabled' person and had forcefully shaped her behaviour and her attitudes to herself ('striving to be well adjusted', stoically enduring pain, accepting without question prescribed treatment) which in essence had become a way of behaving which was untrue to herself. She found attitudes in herself which were the product of these forces such as looking down on people who were disabled unless they acted 'normally'. She came to see that the oppression of women and the oppression of the disabled were part of the same process with its hard-to-resist push towards passivity and dependency. The discovery (and that is not too strong a word) by women who are disabled of the pressures that shape their consciousness and their roles is another example of how many of the most penetrating studies of the experience of disablement come not from concerned professionals but from the conjunction of personal reflections enlarged by ideologies imbedded in the mainstream of social thought.

The making of handicapped children

The manufacture of handicaps in childhood occurs in several ways; through the failure to implement existing technology in the area of preventive medicine; inadequacy of early identification and treatment; segregation and institutionalization of children during school years; the system of classification in medicine and educational psychology (as in the medicalization of deviance where, for example, the role of drug companies in the expansion of 'hyperactivity' may be noted); and in the varied and subtle ways social interaction shapes children into their roles as handicapped children rather than children with a handicap. According to Battle (1974), severe impairment profoundly alters the nature of childhood experiences for not only does the child have to make complex adjustments to his objective disability, but also to his family, specialist, and peer group, and each set of interactions can present potentials for positive or negative self-image and self-esteem. How the child handles issues like dependence-independence may be more critically related to the interactional context than to his primary physical status. Severely mentally handicapped children can be seen as unattractive, unproductive and unrewarding objects of social concern and the way society discharges its minimal obligation to such children may be regarded as a measure of their social value. Cohorting children with broadly similar physical problems into segregated settings may have the cumulative effect of encouraging them to identify with others like themselves who become their primary reference group rather than with their normal peer group. A constant battle has to be waged by parents, teachers and others concerned with the welfare of handicapped children against imposing upon them a double stigma – a handicapped identity.

The un-making of handicap

The first part of this chapter emphasized some of the ways in which our society is engaged in the process of making handicap, both literally and figuratively, and while such a perspective inevitably suggests the darker side of the situation it holds the promise that what is made can be un-made and re-made. It was noted in Chapter 1 that the principal thrust of the professionaliz-ation of handicap has been to abnormalize the handicapped, to create a special category in psychology, sociology and medicine – impaired man; so it requires us to offer proof that disability is not deviance and that handicap is unexceptional. This is not toying with words. It is not a propagandist's plea, inviting collusion and pretence in the sense, 'We know they're different, but let's behave as though they are not'. It involves a personal and public act of cognitive and emotional re-tracking, one which consciously seeks to place the normal aspects of the disabled person at the forefront of one's thinking, a task much easier to write than to practise. It involves discarding cumulative and unhelpful stereotypes, both over-positive and over-negative, in a search for a more authentic mode of perception, reflection and social action. 'Normalization' carries some of these ideas but it is too clinical, and if it had not been pre-empted by another context, 'natural-ization' would serve well to convey my intention.

Cameron (1973), in a study of the 'life satisfactions' of normal and disabled people, found that both groups were very similar in their attitudes to what life had offered, did offer and would offer them in the future. While the disabled group judged their lives as 'more difficult' they did not differ significantly from 'normals' in the ways in which they found life satisfactory. There was some evidence that the disabled group expressed a greater liking for other people than did the normal group, but in general, this study reports the similarities in beliefs, hopes and ideas of both groups. Any contact with disabled people reinforces the picture of connection, similarity and likeness, not of difference or deviance.

Normalization

The enthusiasm for the 'normalization' of the handicapped is part of a wider movement, both democratic and egalitarian, and the supporters of the policies of de-institutionalization, mainstream-ing and community involvement were caught up in an ideological cause to challenge the old asylum, segregated-isolationist per-spectives and policies. Schwartz (1977) has argued that the normalization movement is a guilt-reaction to failed policies rather than a reasoned approach to practical problems and she suggests that shame concerning older practices is forcing disabled and retarded individuals to face a world which accepts the verbal slogans of integration but actually offers 'loss, isolation . . . and denigration'. If it is an ideology, it is one I embrace. If there is shame for the older policies (and current practices, for Ely and Rampton are still too close for comfort) of social isolation and neglect it is a reasonable emotion. The weight of evidence is unmistakable; generations of disabled people have grown up in a world which exercises a tolerant despotism over them and has steadfastly refused to see them as human, preferring super- or sub-human perceptions. While there is a measurable gap between rhetoric and reality in respect of normalization it is none the less the only legitimate guiding principle for public policies and private behaviour.

One example will be given. Catherine Drinkwater (1980) has described how a small group of severely mentally handicapped teenagers from Ely Hospital were taken to live with a group of undergraduates. All had been officially classified as 'unfit to live outside'. They were highly institutionalized, e.g. they did not know what brown bread was, did not know that milk was delivered by a milkman let alone came from a cow, 'they thought the dustman was pinching our bin, and had never seen a raw potato'. They learned to clean the house (in the course of which they discovered that three of the teenagers needed glasses), had cookery lessons, went shopping, chose their own clothes and one learned to work the sewing machine. Problems there were, principally in getting them to make their own decisions. Academic subjects had not been neglected for one of the boys had learned to tell the time, to read a little and to write a letter. This small-scale, but very impressive project has shown that with appropriate help and the right climate some of the most handicapped members of society can find a place, but as Drinkwater points out, possibly the most important message of the project is political, for it costs only about half of what it costs to keep a person in a total institution.

There are many similar advances being made which illustrate that we have not yet begun to explore fully the possibilities of normalization. We are learning, but very slowly.

We have the technology

To the positive advantages of normalization and naturalization, (the right of a place within the community and the right to be treated as unstigmatized), we can add the not inconsiderable benefits of technology. It is hard to underestimate the potential contribution of technology in improving the life of severely disabled children and adults. As examples we can take the portable communication system for the non-verbal severely handicapped person, the POSUM communicator, or the echo-locating system which has been successfully used with blind babies enabling them to locate objects. Bower (1977) describes one of the early experiments on echo-location:

> In many ways the first session was the most exciting of all. An object was introduced and moved slowly to and fro from the baby's face, close enough to tap the baby on the nose. On the

fourth presentation we noticed convergence movements of the eyes . . . on the seventh presentation the baby interposed his hands between face and object. [The session went on to tracking skills and the baby succeeded in hitting a one centimetre cube four times.] His mother stood the baby on her knees at arms' length, chatted to him, telling him what a clever boy he was . . . The baby was facing her and wearing the device. He slowly turned his head to remove her from the sound field, then slowly turned back to bring her in again. [This behaviour was repeated with lots of smiling.] . . . he was playing a kind of peek-a-boo. He was able to identify a favourite toy without touching it. He learned two-handed searches and to search for objects hidden behind another object. (Bower, 1977: 256–7)

Such technology not only supplies an analogue of vision but one which is there at the beginning of the child's development and thus is capable of changing the whole nature of learning inputs which will reshape the cognitive, social and emotional development of the blind infant.

The attempts to match man and machine, as in the case of replacements for amputated limbs, are limited by the amazing versatility of the human limb, making it hard to replicate. Another problem is the control over the new limb and its source of power. The use of signals for the residual portion of the limb to control the prosthetic device may be a new beginning in this type of work. Patient Operator Selector Mechanisms (POSUM) is a system which uses residual physical movements, amplifies and extends them, and harnesses them to the keyboard of an electric typewriter. Micro-switches operated by pressures of three grams or movement of only one-thousandth of an inch mean that a severely paralyzed person can operate an electric car. Wheelchairs that can be controlled by head movements alone and others that can climb stairs are other examples of technical developments. The techniques developed at the Spinal Injuries Unit at Stoke Mandeville Hospital using the powerful muscles of the back have enabled 'spinal man' to sit and walk. So successful has this type of work been that it has been claimed that 'the extent of recovery is no longer the severity of the injury itself but largely the personality and attitude of the patient' (Fishlock, 1969: 107). It

has become apparent that functionally effective prosthetic devices must also have a human dimension. They must be adapted
'physically, aesthetically and psychologically', according to
Fishlock, and must not seriously distort the patient's body image.

These and other technical advances make it increasingly
possible for many of the most impairing aspects of disability to be
ameliorated, but they are not widely available nor cheap enough;
but they will have the long-term effect of allowing the disabled
the possibilities of normal role taking.

Civil rights and protest

The movement from under the umbrella of philanthropy to
something like a civil rights movement has been growing among
the politically-conscious disabled, and their views are spreading.
This movement arose coincidentally with the growing consciousness of disadvantage and stigma in many minority groups – ethnic
minorities, women, gays; an almost identical vocabulary of
protest emerges from them. This vocabulary of protest marks a
significant shift in consciousness from one of almost passive
dependence to active involvement in raising that consciousness
to the point where the minority group is no longer one for whom
pleas, reforms and changes are made by others but where they
themselves are instrumental in provoking change. In many
similar movements with similar pleas for positive discrimination
and normalization, the group has to create a sense of group
identity which, initially, may seem to work against the objective
of removing a feeling of social difference.

It is often said and written that disabled and handicapped
people feel themselves to be in a position not unlike that of an
ethnic minority. This parallel may be seen in the vocabulary of
the National Union of the Deaf, 'We deaf people', and the schools'
for the deaf emphasis on speech is 'pandering to the "white
nigger" syndrome that pretends that deaf children are not really
deaf' and 'we are the truly silent majority'. Deaf people are a
'dependent sub-culture' which had depended on hearing people
speaking for them and now wishes to make its independent
contribution to schooling for hearing-impaired children. The NUD
complains that deafness has been taken over by professionals and

it is demanding a place for the opinions of deaf people about what is the most suitable method and style of learning. This Union believes the voice of the consumer needs to be heard and attended to. In its 'open letter' of May 1978, the NUD argued that the experience of deafness is to experience 'repression and authoritarianism'; the letter goes on to complain that as far as deaf children have been concerned two false gods have been set up – normality and success. The illusion is that the majority of deaf children will learn to talk fluently and be comprehended so that they will achieve social integration. The route to integration is through hard work which leads to success. But as the NUD points out this illusion makes for despair, for only a tiny minority can achieve full integration. The letter concludes:

> It is the first time that we deaf people have addressed you directly with a point of view. Please do not think that we are 'against' you, to use the pitiful point of reference of many hearing professionals. We welcome you as equals . . . We should be allies . . . You are the victims of a subtle brainwashing and a vast subconscious deception that has been deep-rooted in our society ever since the first deaf man was put into an asylum. Please . . . be brave enough to change your views. It does not cost much pride because it is we, deaf people, who are telling you this and you can truly say it is our voice, the voice of the consumer, that has inspired you to understand more fully. (*Open Letter*, NUD, 1978)

The perspective of the able-bodied through which the disabled and impaired were led to normality by training and a gradual change of public attitudes is not perceived by disabled people as either appropriate or successful. Perhaps there is a necessary stage through which those who have been compassionately stigmatized need to go, in which they identify more closely with each other than with the mainstream of society. This is a different form of association from the club and social groups of blind and deaf and physically handicapped people which are shelters from ostracism and more of a political training cadre. The radicalization and politicization of disability seem to me the most promising of portents. We may liken it to a civil rights movement where paternalism, if not eradicated, is no longer seen as a legitimate ideology.

Like the struggle of black people to gain a valid identity, sense of self-esteem and justice, so disabled people are beginning to understand their role in this process. At first their presence was a form of tokenism – the token person in a wheelchair would be wheeled out at conferences to give the 'inside story' which, while listened to with interest, could not change the status of disabled people nor the practices of those in power over them, but it allowed the professional to feel that the shadow if not the substance of democracy was being observed. From that stage we are beginning to move to a place where such contributions are seen not just as interesting anecdotes but as the most significant opinion-forming element in social context of handicap. If there is a watchword for the next decade it is an injunction on professionals to listen to their clients and for disabled people to translate their newly found and hard won insights into an effective political power base from which both parties can begin re-negotiations. The professional interventionist model may have been just another myth.

Backlash

Morris (1980), writing on the International Year of Disabled Persons 1981, noted that there were four main aims set out as a Charter for disabled persons.

1 To save as many people as possible from becoming disabled by maximizing the prevention of disability.
2 To reduce the handicapping effects of disability by adequate rehabilitation services.
3 To ensure that disabled people are part of and not apart from society.
4 To promote full public awareness of the problems of disabled people and of their rights to social equality.

To this list I would like to expand point 3 with this: and to ensure that disabled people acquire a larger share in the decisions that affect them.

However, a cautious note needs to be appended. Dominant majorities like to give themselves a pat on the back when they can demonstrate that they are not so prejudiced as they once were. But they can become irritated and resentful when the suppressed minorities begin their Oliver Twist act and ask for a little more. Frederic Raphael in a review of Edmund White's *States of Desire* gives this view of majority resentment.

> A friend of mine in a wheelchair was warned recently by a well-wisher of a coming backlash against the handicapped. People had had just about enough of their demands for more ramps and special facilities. 'Coming out' with its parading connotations seems to threaten straight society. (Raphael, *The Sunday Times*, 7 September 1980)

Margaret Norris (1978) has noted a change in British social attitudes towards those we like to help. Between 1972 and 1976 she detected an 'increase in negative attitudes towards most groups, including the highly favoured aged and handicapped'. She found her respondents in general to be more sympathetic than hostile, but between these extremes there was a growing middle ground of opinion that help should be selective and limited to 'deserving cases'. The increase in the numbers of unsympathetic responses, (e.g. towards the aged, 31–48, physically handicapped 33–48, mentally handicapped 206–248) suggests that aid giving and receptivity to minorities receiving additional help is related to the general economic climate and since the study was undertaken that climate has deteriorated. We may find that the 1980s are a time when the legitimate ambitions of the disabled and handicapped are confronted by a major shift of popular attitudes and rather than seeing progress in distribution of resources and more positive attitudes we may see a period of stagnation or even reversal.

Models of social repair

Professor Pamela Poppleton (1978) states, 'the kinds of decisions we make about social problems are not pragmatic. They reflect the models we have about the nature of society and social breakdown in particular.'

The interventionist principle can create the illusion of progress and perhaps more than just illusion as long as the economic base of society is expansionist and producing sufficient surplus to enable social repair to take place without imposing undue burdens. The situation may change when the surplus is small (or even nonexistent) and the more positive attitudes towards disadvantaged groups are revealed not as a fundamental shift in social priorities but as a transitional mood liable to sudden fluctuations and reversals. For anything like a substantive shift in attitudes and values we probably need an equivalent restructuring of society.

Many years ago Hanks and Hanks carried out a survey of attitudes and practice towards disabled people in non-Western societies, and in their conclusions offered the following suggestions:

> that the protection of the physically handicapped and social participation for them is *increased* in societies where (1) the level of productivity is higher in proportion to the population and its distribution more nearly equal, (2) competitive factors in individual or group achievement are minimized, (3) the criteria for achievement are not formally absolute as in hierarchical social structures and more weighted with concern for individual capacity as in democratic social structures. (Hanks and Hanks, 1948: 20)

With such criteria the optimism for the next decade must clearly be tempered.

There is one view which I find has a legitimate measure of optimism and which has been well expressed by Tom Crabtree (1980).

> Next year is the International Year of Disabled People and now is a good time to start thinking about the handicapped in our midst. Mind you, I'm never quite sure who they are. There are plenty of walking wounded, the psychologically crippled, who never make it onto any disabled register . . . there are those of us who are far less able to lead a normal life than those who go about in wheelchairs, or who carry white canes, or who need to give themselves daily injections of insulin . . . Your blind friend and that woman with paraplegia may be making a far better job of coping with life than you ever will. It isn't the disability but the adjustment that counts . . . the disabled are just like you and me, brothers and sisters.

References

Agerholm, M. (1973) *Memorandum of the Association of Disabled Professionals: a consultative document on the quota scheme for disabled people*, Department of Employment.

Ashley, J. (1973) *Journey into Silence*, London, The Bodley Head.

Battle, C.U. (1974) 'Disruption in the socialization of a severely handicapped child', *Rehabilitation Literature*, 35, 5, 130–40.

Battye, L. (1966) *I Had a Little Nut Tree*, London, Secker & Warburg.

Beattie, G.W. (1979) 'On becoming an artificial arm user', *New Society*, 48, 510–11.

Berger, P.L. and Luckmann, T. (1971) *The Social Construction of Reality*, Harmondsworth, Penguin Books.

Birenbaum, A. (1970) 'On managing a courtesy stigma', *Journal of Health and Social Behavior*, 11, 196–206.

Birenbaum, A. (1971) 'The mentally retarded child in the home and family cycle', *Journal of Health and Social Behavior*, 12, 55–65.

Blaxter, M. (1976) *The Meaning of Disability*, London, Heinemann.

Boles, G. (1959) 'Personality factors in mothers of cerebral palsied children', *Genetic Psychology Monograph*, 59, 160–218.

Booth, T.A. (1978) 'From normal baby to handicapped child', *Sociology*, 12, 2, 203–21.

Bossard, J.H.S. and Boll, E.S. (1960) *The Sociology of Child Development*, New York, Harper & Row.

Bowe, F. (1978) *Handicapping America*, New York, Harper & Row.

Bower, T. (1977) 'Blind babies see with their ears', *New Scientist*, 3, 2, 255–7.

Bowlby, J. (1960) 'Separation anxiety', *International Journal of Psycho-Analysis*, 41, 69–113.

Bowlby, J. (1969) *Attachment*, London, The Hogarth Press.

Brock, M. (1975) *Christopher: a silent life*, London, Macmillan.

Brooks, V.W. (1956) *Helen Keller*, London, J.M. Dent.

Brown, C. (1972) *The Childhood Story of Christy Brown*, London, Pan Books.

Browning, E. (1972) *I Can't See What You're Saying*, London, Paul Elek.

Bury, M.R. (1979) 'Disablement in society', *International Journal of*

Rehabilitation Research, 2, 1, 34–40.

Cameron, P. (1973) 'The life satisfactions of non-normal persons', *Journal of Consulting and Clinical Psychology*, 41, 3, 207–14.

Campling, J. (1979) *Better Lives for Disabled Women*, London, Virago.

Campling, J. (ed.) (1981) *Images of Ourselves: women with disabilities talking*, London, Routledge & Kegan Paul.

Cockburn, J. (1980) 'Why James Haig decided on suicide', *The Observer*, 31 August, 5.

Cohen, S. and Taylor, L. (1972) *Psychological Survival*, Harmondsworth, Penguin Books.

Conley, R.W. (1974) 'Economics and retardation', *Social & Rehabilitation Record*, 1, 10, 20–5.

Consumers' Association (1974) *Coping with Disablement*, London, The Consumers' Association.

Cooke, S. (1979) *Ragged Owlet*, London, Arrow Books.

Court Report (1976) *Fit for the Future: report of the committee on child health services*, London, HMSO.

Coveney, P. (1967) *The Image of Childhood*, Harmondsworth, Penguin Books.

Crabtree, T. (1980) 'I know very few people who aren't disabled', *The Guardian*, 8 August, 9.

Craig, M. (1979) *Blessings*, London, Hodder & Stoughton.

Cruickshank, W. (1952) 'A study of the relation of physical disability to social adjustment', *American Journal of Occupational Therapy*, 3, 100–9.

Cummings, S.T. (1976) 'The impact of the child's deficiency on the father', *American Journal of Orthopsychiatry*, 46, 2, 246–55.

Dalton, M.E. and Dalton, K. (1978) 'Handicapped sex', *New Society*, 28 September, 698.

Darling, R.B. (1979) *Families Against Society*, Beverley Hills, Calif., Sage Publications.

Davis, F. (1964) 'Deviance disavowal; the management of strained interactions by the visibly handicapped', in Becker, H.S. (ed.) *The Other Side*, New York, The Free Press.

Deacon, J. (1974) *Tongue-tied: fifty years of friendship in a subnormality hospital*, London, National Society for Mentally Handicapped Children.

Dean, V. (1957) *Three Steps Forward*, London, Faber & Faber.

Department of Health and Social Security, *Aids for Disabled People*, HB2, DHSS.

Dodge, J.A. (1974) 'The size of the problem', in Burton, L. (ed.) *Care of the Child Facing Death*, London, Routledge & Kegan Paul.

Drimmer, F. (1976) *Very Special People: the struggles, loves and triumphs of human oddities*, New York, Bantam Books.

Drinkwater, C. (1980) 'Life on the outside with mental handicap', *New Society*, 23 October, 164–5.

Edwards, G. (1962) *Keep in Touch*, St Alban's, Herts, MacGibbon & Kee.

Ellis, H.J. (1974) 'Parental involvement in the decision to treat spina bifida cystica', *British Medical Journal*, 1, 369–72.

Epilepsy Congress (1977) 'A new look at life by people with epilepsy', *Epilepsy International*.

Epstein, J. (1968) *Mermaid on Wheels*, London, Hubert Jackson.

Euroforum (1980) 'Can life be made easier for the handicapped?', Editorial, *Euroforum*, October, 3–4.

Evans, M. (1978) *A Ray of Darkness*, London, John Calder.

Faircloth, S. (1981) 'Disability Action', *New Society*, 2 July, 19.

Farber, B. (1959) 'Effects of a severely retarded child on family integration', *Social Research Child Development Monograph*, 24, 2.

Filstead, W.J. (ed.) (1973) *An Introduction to Deviance*, Chicago, Rand McNally.

Finkelstein, V. (1980) *Attitude and Disabled People*, New York, World Rehabilitation Fund.

Fishlock, D. (1969) *Man Modified*, London, Jonathan Cape.

Fox, A.M. (1974) *They Get This Training But They Don't Really Know How You Feel*, Action Research for the Crippled Child.

Fraiberg, S. (1977) *Insights from the Blind*, London, Souvenir Press.

Frazer, Lord Lonsdale (1961) *My Story of St. Dunstan's*, London, Harrap.

Garrard, J. (1974) 'Impairment, and disability: their management, prevalence and psychological cost', in Lees, D.S. and Shaw, S. (eds) *Impairment, Disability and Handicap*, London, Heinemann.

Gath, A. (1974) 'Sibling reaction to mental handicap', *Journal of Child Psychology and Psychiatry*, 15, 187–93.

Gibson, D. (1978) *Down's Syndrome: the psychology of mongolism*, Cambridge, Cambridge University Press.

Gliedeman, J. and Roth, W. (1980) *The Unexpected Minority*, New York, Harcourt Brace Jovanovich.

Goffman, E. (1961) *Asylums*, New York, Doubleday.

Goffman, E. (1963) *Stigma*, Englewood Cliffs, N.J., Prentice Hall.

Goodstein, L.D. (1960) 'MMPI differences between parents of children with cleft palates and parents of physically normal children', *Journal of Speech and Hearing Research*, 3, 31–8.

Gould, D. (1972) 'A baby doomed to live', *New Statesman*, 27 October, 585.

Green, M. (1966) *Elizabeth: a mentally handicapped daughter*, London, Hodder & Stoughton.

Greengross, W. (1976) *Entitled to Love: the sexual and emotional needs of the handicapped*, Horsham, Sussex, National Fund for Research into Crippling Diseases.

Gregory, S. (1976) *The Deaf Child and his Family*, London, Allen & Unwin.

Haffter, C. (1968) 'The Changeling: history and psychodynamics of attitudes to handicapped children', *Journal of the History of the Behavioral Sciences*, 4, 55–61.

Hale, G. (ed.) (1979) *The Source Book for the Disabled*, London, Paddington Press.

Hales, A. (1978) *The Children of Skylark Ward*, Cambridge, Cambridge University Press.

Hall, D. and Stacey, M. (eds) (1979) *Beyond Separation*, London, Routledge & Kegan Paul.

Hanks, J.R. and Hanks, L.M. (1948) 'The physically handicapped in certain non-occidental countries', *Journal of Social Issues*, 4, 11–20.

Harris, A.I. (1971) *Handicapped and Impaired in Great Britain*, Office of Population, Censuses and Surveys, Survey Division, London, HMSO.

Harrison, R.M. and West, P. (1977) 'Images of a *grand mal*', *New Society*, 12 May, 282.

Hauerwas, S. (1975) 'The demands and limits of care', *The American Journal of the Medical Sciences*, 269, 222–36.

Hay, W. (1754) *Deformity: an essay*, London, R. & J. Dodsley, B.M. General Catalogue of Printed Books, 2314:10.

Herbert, H. (1977) 'One firm in five shuns the disabled', *The Guardian*, 22 May, 14.

Hewett, S. (1970) *The Family and the Handicapped Child*, London, Allen & Unwin.

Hewitt, M. (1981) *A Survey of the Experiences and Perceived Needs of Parents of Handicapped Children*, unpublished diploma dissertation, University of Liverpool.

Hill, A. (1976) *Closed World of Love*, London, Shepherd-Walwyn.

Hoeven, V.J. (1965) *Slant-eyed Angel*, Gerrards Cross, Bucks., Colin Smythe.

Hunt, P. (1966) *Stigma: the experience of disability*, London, Geoffrey Chapman.

Isaacs, B., Livingstone, M. and Neville, Y. (1972) *Survival of the Unfittest: a study of geriatric patients in Glasgow*, London, Routledge & Kegan Paul.

James, C. (1979) *The Observer*, 10 May, 20.

Jones, C. (1975) *Opening the Door*, London, Routledge & Kegan Paul.

Katz, I. (1978) 'When courtesy offends: effects of positive and negative behaviours by the physically handicapped on altruism and anger in normals', *Journal of Personality*, 46, 506–18.

Keller, H. (1930) *The Story of My Life*, London, Hodder & Stoughton.

Kerr, N. (1977) 'Staff expectations for the disabled person', in Stubbins, J. (ed.) *Social and Psychological Aspects of Disability*, Baltimore, University Park Press.

Kew, S. (1975) *Handicap and Family Crisis*, London, Pitman.

King, R.D., Reynes, N.V. and Tizard, J. (1971) *Patterns of Residential Care*, London, Routledge & Kegan Paul.

Kleck, R. (1968) 'Physical stigma and non-verbal cues emitted in face to face situations', *Human Relations*, 21, 1, 19–28.

Krebs, D.L. (1970) 'Altruism: an examination of the concept and a review of the literature', *Psychological Bulletin*, 73, 4, 258–312.

Landvater, D. (1976) *David*, Englewood Cliffs, NJ, Prentice Hall.

Laslett, P. (1977) *Family Life and Illicit Love in Earlier Generations*, Cambridge, Cambridge University Press.

Lees, D. and Shaw, S. (eds) (1974) *Impairment, Disability and Handicap*, London, Heinemann.

Lethbridge, C. (1974) *By Accident*, London, Hodder & Stoughton.

Lovell, A. (1978) *In a Summer Garment: the experience of an autistic boy*, London, Secker & Warburg.

Lowman, E.W. and Klinger, J.L. (1969) *Aids to Independent Living*, New York, McGraw-Hill.

Lukoff, I.F. (1972) *Attitudes Towards Blind Persons*, American Foundation for the Blind.

McCormack, M. (1978) *A Mentally Handicapped Child in the Family: a guide for parents*, London, Constable.

McMichael, J. (1971) *Handicap: a study of physically handicapped children and their families*, St Albans, Herts., Crosby Lockwood Staples.

Marais, E. (1978) 'Peter: no escape from a locked ward', *New Society*, 2 November, 268–9.

Mason, D. (1976) *Thalidomide: my fight*, London, Allen & Unwin.

Miller, E.J. and Gwynne, G.V. (1972) *A Life Apart*, London, Tavistock.

Miller, R. (1977) 'Unlocking the doors', *The Sunday Times Magazine*, 13 March, 32–42.

Minde, K.S. (1972) 'How they grow up; forty-one physically handicapped children and their families', *American Journal of Psychiatry*, 128, 1554–60.

Minton, H.G. (1974) *Blind Man's Buff*, London, Paul Elek.

Mittler, P. (1979) *People not Patients*, London, Methuen.

Morris, A. (1978) 'The disabled worker', DHSS and DoE Letter.

Morris, A. (1980) '500 million lives at stake', *The Sunday Times*, 21 September, 21.

Moss, P. and Silver, O. (1972) *Mentally Handicapped Schoolchildren and Their Families*, Liverpool Education Committee and London University Child Development Unit.

Motte, P. and Motte, N. (1956) *The Hand of the Potter*, London, Cassell.

Munday, D. (1976) *Dorcas: opportunity not pity*, Tunbridge Wells, Kent, Midas Books.

Musgrove, F. (1977) *Margins of the Mind*, London, Methuen.

Mussett, H. (1975) *The Untrodden Way*, London, Gollancz.

National Children's Bureau (1976) *Help Starts Here*, London, National Children's Bureau.

National Union of the Deaf (1978) 'Open letter', *Teacher of the Deaf*, 2, 3, 6–8.

National Union of Students (1976) *The Disabled Student*, Horsham, Sussex, Action Research for the Crippled Child.

Newton, E. (1980) *This Bed My Centre*, London, Virago.

Opie, I. and Opie, P. (1959) *The Lore and Language of Schoolchildren*, Oxford, Oxford University Press.

Oswin, M. (1971) *The Empty Hours*, London, Allen Lane.

Park, C.C. (1967) *The Siege*, London, Pelican Books.

Parsons, T. (1951) *The Social System*, New York, The Free Press.

Pill, R. (1979) 'Status and career; a sociological approach to the study of child patients', in Hall, D. and Stacey, M. (eds) *Beyond Separation*, London, Routledge & Kegan Paul.

Poppleton, P. (1978) 'Models of social repair: myths and dilemmas', in Armytage, W.H.G. and Peel, J. (eds) *Perimeters of Social Repair*, London, Academic Press.

Potter, D. (1975) 'Dog on a chain', *New Society*, 20 March, 735–6.

Rackham, K. (1975) 'The role of boarding schools in the treatment of children with recurrent disabling conditions', *Child: care, health and development*, 1, 19–27.

Raphael, F. (1980) *The Sunday Times*, 7 September, 42.

Reynolds, S. (1980) 'Did you hear the one about Miss Disabled Beauty?' *The Guardian*, 28 August, 10.

Robb, B. (1967) *Sans Everything*, Sunbury-on-Thames, Thomas Nelson.

Roskies, E. (1972) *Abnormality and Normality: the mothering of thalidomide children*, New York, Cornell University Press.

Schwartz, C. (1977) 'Normalization and idealism', *Mental Retardation*, 15, 38–9.

Scott, E., Jan, J.E. and Freeman, R.D. (1977) *Can't Your Child See?* Baltimore, University Park Press.

Scott, R.A. (1969) *The Making of Blind Men*, New York, Russell Sage Foundation.

Shakespeare, R. (1973) *The Psychology of Handicap*, London, Methuen.

Sheridan, M. (1973) *The Handicapped Child and his Home*, London, National Children's Home.

Simkins, J. and Tickner, V. (1978) *Whose Benefit? Uncertainties of Cash Benefits for the Handicapped*, London, The Economist Intelligence Unit.

Snowdon Report (1976) *Integrating the Disabled*, Horsham, Sussex, National Fund for Research into Crippling Diseases.

Sontag, S. (1972) 'The double standard of ageing', *Saturday Review*, 29–38.

Stein, Z.A. (1975) 'Strategies for the prevention of mental retardation', *Bulletin of the New York Academy of Medicine*, 51, 1, 130–42.

Stigen, G. (1976) *Heartaches and Handicaps: an irreverent survival manual for parents*, Palo Alto, Calif., Science and Behavior Books.

Strong, P.M. (1979) *The Ceremonial Order of the Clinic: patients, doctors and the medical bureaucracies*, London, Routledge & Kegan Paul.

Stubbins, J. (ed.) (1977) *Social and Psychological Aspects of Disability*, Baltimore, University Park Press.

Tajfel, H. (1978) *The Social Psychology of Minorities*, London, Minority Rights Group, Report no. 38.

Thomas, E.J. (1970) 'Problems of disability from the perspective of role theory', in Glasser, P.H. and Glasser, L.N. (eds) *Families in Crisis*, New York, Harper & Row.

Thomas, K. (1977) 'The place of laughter in Tudor and Stuart England', *The Times Literary Supplement*, 21 January, 77–81.

Titmuss, R.M. (1970) *The Gift Relationship*, London, Allen & Unwin.

Tizard, J. and Grad, J.C. (1961) *The Mentally Handicapped and Their Families*, Oxford, Oxford University Press.

Tizard, J. and Tizard, B. (1974) 'The institution as an environment for development', in Richards, M.P.M. (ed.) *The Integration of the Child into a Social World*, Cambridge, Cambridge University Press, 137–52.

Toynbee, P. (1978) *Hospital*, London, Hutchinson.

Trust, D. (1978) *Skin Deep*, Edinburgh, Paul Harris.

Vadja, A. (1974) *Lend Me an Eye*, London, Paul Elek.

Villey, P. (1930) *The World of the Blind*, London, Gerald Duckworth.

Vischer, A.L. (1978) 'On growing old', in Carver, V. and Liddiard, P. (eds) *An Ageing Population*, Sevenoaks, Kent, Hodder & Stoughton (in association with the Open University).

Voysey, M. (1975) *A Constant Burden*, London, Routledge & Kegan Paul.

Wallace, M. and Robson, M. (1976) *On Giant's Shoulders*, London, Times Books.

Welch, D. (1966) *A Voice Through the Clouds*, London, Faber & Faber.

Wells, T. (1978) 'On the receiving end', *The Times Educational Supplement*, 10 November, 21.

West, P. (1970) *Words for a Deaf Daughter*, New York, Harper & Row.

Wilks, J. and Wilks, E. (1974) *Bernard: bringing up our mongol son*, London, Routledge & Kegan Paul.

Woodburn, M. (1972) *Social implications of Spina Bifida*, Windsor, Berks., National Foundation for Educational Research.

Worthington, M.E. (1977) 'Personal space as a function of the stigma effect', in Stubbins, J. (ed.) *Social and Psychological Aspects of Disability*, Baltimore, University Park Press.

Wright, H. (1978) 'Down blind alleys', *The Guardian*, 31 October, 9.

Wynn, M. and Wynn, A. (1979) *Prevention of Handicap and the Health of Women*, London, Routledge & Kegan Paul.

Additional references

Anderson, E. (1973) *The Disabled Schoolchild*, London, Methuen.

Baskin, B.H. and Harris, K.H. (1977) *Notes from a Different Drummer: a guide to juvenile fiction portraying the handicapped*, New York, R.R. Bowker.

Blackhall, D.S. (1971) *The Way I See It*, London, John Baker.

Blackley, R. (1974) *Despite Disability*, Reading, Berks., Educational Explorers.

Blaisdell, A. (1968) *Something Wrong*, London, Victor Gollancz

Buck, P.S. (1951) *The Child who Never Grew*, London, Methuen.

Carling, F. (1958) *And Yet We are Human*, London, Chatto & Windus.

Copeland, J. (1973) *For the Love of Ann*, London, Arrow Books.

De Vries-Kruyt, T. (1971) *Small Ship, Great Sea*, London, Collins.

Elliott, R. (1971) *Life and Leisure for the Physically Handicapped*, London, Paul Elek.

Forsythe, E. (1979) *Living with Muscular Dystrophy*, London, Faber & Faber.

Higgins, E.T. (1969) *Still Life*, Oxford, A.R. Mowbray.

Hitchford, J. (1973) *Eyes at my Feet*, London, Michael Joseph.

Hocken, S. (1978) *Emma and I*, London, Sphere Books.

Hunt, N. (1967) *The World of Nigel Hunt*, Chichester, Sussex, Darwen Finlayson.

Lorenz, S.E. (1969) *Our Son, Ken*, New York, Dell.

McDaniel, J.W. (1969) *Physical Disability and Behaviour*, Oxford, Pergamon.

Murphy, G.E.B. (1956) *Your Deafness is Not You*, Tadworth, Surrey, The World's Work.

Neal, E. (1961) *One of Those Children*, London, Allen & Unwin.

Pellow, J. and Bates, P. (1964) *Horizontal Man*, London, Longmans.

Rorvick, D.M. (1971) *As Man Becomes Machine*, London, Souvenir Press.

Rowan, P. (1980) *What Sort of Life?* Windsor, Berks., National Foundation for Educational Research.

Sarno, J.E. and Sarno, M.T. (1979) *Stroke*, New York, McGraw-Hill.

Stone, J. and Taylor, F. (1977) *A Handbook for Parents with a Handicapped Child*, London, Arrow Books.

Topliss, E. (1975) *Provision for the Disabled*, Oxford, Basil Blackwell.

Wakefield, T. (1978) *Some Mothers I Know*, London, Routledge & Kegan Paul.

White, R. (1972) *Be Not Afraid*, London, The Bodley Head.

Index

adolescence, 153, 157–8
adventitious handicap, 39
ageing, 88–90
Agerholm, M., 8
Aids for the Disabled, 88
Aids to Independent Living, 88
altruism, 72
amniocentesis, 176–7
Aristotle, 22
Ashley, Jack, 41–2, 65–6
Asylums, 73
attachment behaviour, 143
attitudes: to handicap, 21–4, 37
autism, 99, 133–6, 140
A Voice Through a Cloud, 50
Axline, V., 150

backlash, 191–2
Bacon, Sir Francis, 23–4
barriers, 177–82
Battle, C.U., 184
Battye, Louis, 66, 155–6
Beattie, G.W., 44–5
beneficiary: status of, 64
Berger, P.L., 4
Bernard: Bringing up our Mongol Son, 141
Bettelheim, B., 150
Better Lives for Disabled Women, 183
Birenbaum, A., 101, 119, 140, 142
Blaxter, M., 4

blindness, 60–1, 64–5, 76–8, 159–60
Boles, G., 102
Boll, E.S., 71
bonding, 71
Booth, T.A., 102, 119–20
Bossard, J.H.S., 71
Bowe, F., 22, 177–81
Bower, T., 187–8
Bowlby, J., 71, 143
Braille, 77
British Epilepsy Association, 46
Brock, M., 146–7
Brooks, V.W., 29, 30
Brown, Christy, 162
Browning, Elizabeth, 132–3, 144
Bury, M.R., 6, 7

Cameron, P., 186
Campling, J., 182–3
caregiving, 71–4
caretaking, 74–8
Centre for the Disabled, 82
cerebral palsy, 155, 176
Cheshire Home, 82–4
childhood, 84–5, 150–3
Christopher, 146
Chronically Sick and Disabled Persons Act (1970), 180–2
civil rights, 189–91
Closed World of Love, 147
Cohen, S., 85
committee on sexual and